Also by Julia Child

Mastering the Art of French Cooking, Volume I
(with Simone Beck and Louisette Bertholle)

The French Chef Cookbook

Mastering the Art of French Cooking, Volume II
(with Simone Beck)

From Julia Child's Kitchen

The Way to Cook

Cooking with Master Chefs

In Julia's Kitchen with Master Chefs

Julia's Delicious Little Dinners

Julia's Delicious Little Dinners

by Julia Child

In collaboration with E. S. Yntema

Photographs by James Scherer

Alfred A. Knopf   New York   1998

This Is a Borzoi Book
Published by Alfred A. Knopf, Inc.

Copyright © 1998 by Julia Child
All rights reserved under International and Pan-American Copyright Conventions. Published in the United States by Alfred A. Knopf, Inc., New York, and simultaneously in Canada by Random House of Canada Limited, Toronto. Distributed by Random House, Inc., New York.
www.randomhouse.com

The recipes in this book were originally published in the books *Julia Child & Company* and *Julia Child & More Company,* which were published by Alfred A. Knopf, Inc., in 1978 and 1979 respectively. Copyright © 1978 (*Julia Child & Company*) and copyright © 1979 (*Julia Child & More Company*) by Julia Child. These two books were also released in a single edition as *Julia Child's Menu Cookbook,* published in 1991 by Wings Books, distributed by Outlet Book Company, Inc., a Random House Company, by arrangement with Alfred A. Knopf, Inc.

"Dinner for the Boss" and "Butterflied Pork for a Party" both appeared in somewhat shorter form in *McCall's.*

Library of Congress Cataloging-in-Publication Data
Child, Julia.
Julia's delicious little dinners / by Julia Child in collaboration with E. S. Yntema ; photographs by James Scherer. — 1st ed.
p.   cm.
Includes index.
ISBN 0-375-40336-1
1. Dinners and dining.   2. Cookery.   3. Menus.
I. Yntema, E. S.   II. Title.
TX739.C464   1998
642'.4—dc21   98-6376
                              CIP

Manufactured in the United States of America
First Edition

Contents

Acknowledgments

This is a book of menus drawn from our television series *Julia Child & Company* and its sequel, *Julia Child & More Company*. The recipes for the complete series appeared in two separate books, were then all collected into one big book, and are now split into four convenient smaller books, of which this is the first volume.

The series was produced for public television at WGBH TV in Boston, with Russell Morash as producer/director in association with Ruth Lockwood. The food designer and recipe developer was Rosemary Manell, who worked closely with our photographer, James Scherer. Marian Morash, chef for the popular *This Old House,* was also executive chef for us. I count us fortunate indeed to have had E. S. Yntema as a writer. Peggy Yntema's wit and spirit always make for good reading.

It takes a peck of people to put on shows such as these, and other members of our team at one time or another included Gladys Christopherson, Bess Coughlin, Wendy Davidson, Bonnie Eleph, Jo Ford, Temi Hyde, Sara Moulton, Pat Pratt, John Reardon, Bev Seamons, and, of course, our able makeup artist, Louise Miller. I have not mentioned the technicians, camera crew, and lighting engineers, or our book designer, Chris Pullman, or our favorite editor at Knopf, Judith Jones.

Introduction

Six is a nicely manageable number of guests when you want a really delicious little dinner that shows off your skills but does not overwhelm either you or your kitchen, and this little book is here to help you. Suppose you have invited dear food-loving and wine-savvy friends for a meal and you will center it around a luxury main course—a rack of lamb. What to serve with it, how to begin the meal, and how can you best fit it all into your schedule?

Those are the questions this menu book is designed to answer. Here you have the whole menu set out before you, with an artichoke appetizer, the vegetables to garnish the lamb, the dessert, and the wines. You are given marketing details, a list of staples to have on hand, and specific ingredients for this particular menu. Helpful full-color photographs picture the assembled ingredients as well as the finished dishes, and process shots, such as those for trimming the rack, describe how to go about specific tasks.

It's all here, including a suggested order of battle listing what you can prepare entirely or partially ahead, and what you should save for the last minute. In addition, you are given a choice of variations. If you'd rather have something other than shellfish with the artichokes, for instance, how about minced marinated fresh mushrooms, or fish salad? Or forget artichokes and serve fresh asparagus vinaigrette. Again, maybe you definitely want lamb but not the expensive rack of lamb, so you could then give them the homey yet always welcome stuffed breast of lamb for a quarter of the price, and a full recipe is included.

These are very varied menus, from butterflied pork loin and all its trimmings to an old-fashioned chicken dinner featuring "Hen Bonne Femme," and a cool summer supper of poached salmon steaks, hollandaise sauce, and sautéed cucumbers. All are fully illustrated and annotated as described for the racks of lamb above, and all are designed for the enthusiastic home cook.

We cooks very much enjoyed creating, cooking, and feasting upon these menus, and we hope you will, too.

Bon appétit!

Julia Child

1998

◑ *indicates stop here*
▼ *indicates further discussion under Remarks*

Julia's Delicious Little Dinners

*An impressive dinner for guests who like
their food conservative and luxurious;
and a dissertation on choosing, trimming, and roasting fine beef.*

Dinner for the Boss

Menu
For 6 people

Consommé Brunoise
Melba Toast

❦

Standing Rib Roast of Beef
Timbale of Fresh Corn
Brussels Sprouts Tossed in Butter

❦

Macédoine of Fruits in Champagne
Bourbon-soaked Chocolate Truffles

❦

Suggested wines:
A fine full-bodied Burgundy or Pinot Noir;
Champagne with dessert

What I mean at the moment by "boss," you might mean by the queen of England or the chairman of the Membership Committee: a formidable personage (a) whom you want to impress and (b) whose taste in food runs to the conservative, the expensive, and the simple. For somebody like that, I think automatically of roast beef. Like the "Blue Danube," it may be square, but it's wonderful and everybody loves it. Before spending all that money, though, we ought to know a few things about the choosing and roasting of beef. However, roast beef isn't the only possible choice for the boss, so, in case it is too expensive for you, I have listed a number of other ideas in Menu Variations, farther on.

Speaking of menus, I all but fell into an elementary planning error myself when I did this meal. I wanted to end it with a knockout blow, like a soufflé, and was mooning over the extravagances of Escoffier: Soufflé à la Régence? à la Reine? Rothschild? Sans-Souci? Vésuvienne? But, running an imaginary tongue over the succession of dishes, I tasted an over-richness, an imbalance…anyway, something wrong. The soufflé on top of the timbale was the trouble, I realized: eggs twice. It wrecks a menu to repeat ingredients, so I eliminated the soufflé.

As for the timbale, I never even used to consider recipes that called for grated fresh corn. It was just too much work to run a knife point down every single row on the ear and then to scrape out the milk and pulp with the back of the blade. Then my brother-in-law gave me a wooden corn scraper one Christmas, and, mad to use it, I discovered that fresh corn was available almost all year round. I confess I had never looked at it before—dismissing it as inedible out of the summer season. But I found it delicious when scraped off the cob with my new grater and turned into cream-style dishes. I also discovered that there are a number of scraper gadgets on the market, mostly available through mail-order catalogues for country-store-type places.

Then, given the warm colors and flavors of the beef and the corn, I wanted a strong-tasting, unstarchy green vegetable with some crunch—so, Brussels sprouts. Green, I say; and crunchy, I insist. Overcooking has given the cabbage family a bad odor and a bad name. Apropos, I remember a story about my old *maître,* Chef Max Bugnard, who did one stage of his classic apprenticeship at a station hotel in London where, he related, cabbage was boiled for several hours, drained, piled into a round platter, and formed into a solid cake by jamming it hard against the kitchen wall. Then this cabbage cake was placed in a steamer and sliced into wedges on demand. Chef said it was years before he could bear boiled cabbage again, or any member of the cabbage family,

for that matter. I thought of him in our TV studio when our director wanted a boiling pot on the stove; we didn't think to change the water after lifting out our Brussels sprouts, and pretty soon a dismal reek, familiar from bad old days and bad old hotels, began to overwhelm the fresh aromas of corn and beef. The smell bore no relation to the briefly boiled emerald-green sprouts awaiting their final toss in hot butter; it simply proved once again that overboiling the cabbage family produces nauseating results.

Green, red, and gold on the plate, the sprouts, beef, and corn demand a pretty dessert. Something cool and delicate, too, not puddingy after the timbale, but something inviting to the tooth. So, I thought, fruit—with a splash of Champagne for tingle. The sparkling macédoine's name, incidentally, means any kind of a combination of fruits—or vegetables—from Alexander of Macedon, whose vast empire included so many disparate populations.

The consommé, though it comes first, was my last decision. Something light before beef, something classic to please the boss, something hot and savory to kindle a good appetite. The brunoise garnish of minced vegetables looks like a scattering of jewels and adds a fresh flavor to the strong winy broth. A pleasantly crisp accompaniment when you don't want anything buttery like cheese straws is homemade Melba toast. The only difficulty with that, however, is finding a loaf of plain nonsweet white sandwich bread that is unsliced. The last time I traipsed all over town to find unsliced bread, I realized I would have saved myself time and energy had I made my own!

The truffles (so called because they look vaguely like the rare underground fungus sniffed out by special dogs—sometimes pigs—in the oak groves of Périgord and sold like diamonds to bosses and their ilk) were not a decision but a fantasy. They are fun to make and unctuous to the tongue: a luxurious final touch.

Preparations

Recommended Equipment:
A corn scraper, as previously mentioned, is virtually essential for the timbale recipe.

Marketing and Storage:
Staples to have on hand

Salt
Peppercorns
Hot pepper sauce or Cayenne pepper
Grated cheese
Fresh bread crumbs
Unsalted butter (½ pound or 225 g)
Eggs (6)
Heavy cream (½ pint or ¼ L)
Onions (6)
Carrots (6)
Garlic
Fresh parsley and/or other fresh herbs
Bay leaves
Dried thyme
Wines and liqueurs: Port, Madeira, or sherry;
    dry white wine or dry white French ver-
    mouth; bourbon whiskey or dark
    Jamaica rum

Specific ingredients for this menu
Prime roast of beef, fully trimmed (3 to 5 ribs)
Consommé (2 quarts or liters)
Unsliced nonsweet white sandwich bread, 1
    day old (1 loaf)
Gingersnaps, best quality (6 ounces or 180 g)
Semisweet baking chocolate (7 ounces or 200 g)
Unsweetened baking chocolate (1 ounce or 30 g)
Unsweetened cocoa powder (½ cup or
    2 ounces, or 60 g)
Instant coffee (¼ cup or 1 ounce, or 30 g)
Celery (2 stalks)
Leeks (2)
White turnips (2)
Fresh green beans (¼ pound or 115 g)
Fresh corn (12 to 14 ears)
Fresh fine Brussels sprouts (two to three 10-
    ounce or 285-g packages)
Fruits for the dessert (see recipe)
Ripe tomatoes (1)
Champagne for dessert (2 bottles)

How to Buy and Trim a Rib Roast of Beef

A rib roast comes from one side of the steer's back and includes the ribs from the primal (wholesaler's) "rib" cut only. As you can see from the drawing, the ribs are cut off at two-thirds their length from the backbone (or chine, pronounced "shine").

The primal cut looks like this (opposite, left) when it comes from the wholesaler to your butcher. Nothing has been removed but the hide.

On the fat, notice the purple U.S. Department of Agriculture grade stamp. This particular cut is stamped Prime, or top quality, which means that the beef has firm, pale fat and that the lean is bright red and well marbled. Marbling refers to the white web of fat diffused in three dimensions throughout the lean. The meat has a tender, close-grained, glossy texture. Not all butchers carry top-quality, Prime beef since it is in great demand by hotels and restaurants. (Incidentally, the term "prime rib roast of beef" refers to the beef quality, not to the ribs themselves.) The next grade of beef is labeled Choice and is very good, too, although not as heavy and not as marbled. Frankly, I would not buy a beef roast at all if it were not at least Choice in grade; I would pick another cut or kind of meat.

Under the thick outer layer of fat lie two thinnish pieces, called "cap meat," which though sometimes left on should really be removed since they are for pot-roasting.

The short rib ends should be sawed off close to the end of the rib-eye meat. The ends nearest the shoulder are trimmed of excess fat and may be braised; the others, with less meat, are scraped clean and the meat is used for hamburger. The backbone or chine should be sawed off and all vestiges of it removed for ease in carving. There is also a tough nerve running along the top outside edge, which should be cut out.

Here is a cross section of a rib roast showing the differences between the small or loin end, with its solid eye of meat, and the large or shoulder end. Note that the meat from the shoulder end shows separations and that the eye of the roast is smaller. Note also the cap of meat under the top layer of fat; you are paying roast beef prices for stew meat here.

In other words, the choice end of the roast is the small end; you should know what you are asking for and call it by the right name. If you say you want "the first four ribs," you have made a meaningless and confusing request since ribs are officially numbered from the neck or shoulder end. Ribs numbers 1 through 5 are part of the shoulder. Ribs numbers 6 through 12 are part of the rib roast, and the ribs nearest the loin are the ones you want: numbers 12, 11, 10, 9, and 8—if you want a 5-rib roast. You can also request "a roast from the small end," but you are safer specifying both "small end" and rib numbers.

This is a 5-rib roast from the small end, ribs 8 through 12, trimmed and ready for the

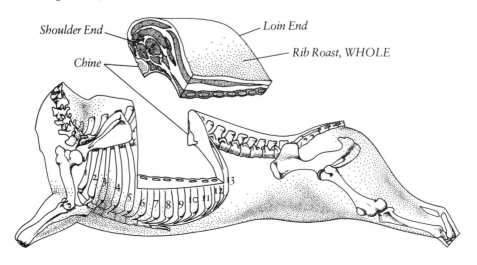

Shoulder End

Loin End

Chine

Rib Roast, WHOLE

oven. It is a Prime roast, weighs 11½ pounds (5¼ kg), and takes 2½ hours in a 325°F/170°C oven—or some 13 minutes per pound—for the internal temperature at the small (loin) end to reach 120°F/49°C, meaning that the loin half will be pinky-red rare, and the large end red rare. It will serve 14 to 16 people. So why buy such a large roast for 6 people when a 3-rib roast would do? Well, if I am going to have a roast of beef at all, I like a big one, since I can use it twice for guests, once hot and once cold. And any leftovers will provide a plush family meal, sliced and carefully reheated in foil.

Meat Temperatures:

We like rare beef in our family, and I find that 120°F/49°C at the small end is just right for us. That means the temperature before the beef is removed from the oven, since it gradually goes up when you take the roast out and soon reaches 130°F/54°C because the hot juices at the outside layer of meat recirculate into the interior, raising the temperature accordingly. Please note, however, that a temperature of 140°F/60°C before the roast is taken out of the oven—meaning 5 minutes or so longer per pound or half kilo, and a pinky-gray color—is considered the "safe" temperature for cooked meats, where salmonella and other sick-making bacteria are surely killed off. Thus we rare-meat lovers eat red beef at our own peril and should be sure of our butchers, restaurateurs, and other purveyors of raw and/or rare beef.

Speaking of temperatures, I do think an accurate meat thermometer is essential for the home cook, and the instant or microwave oven thermometer is available in most good cookware shops; put it in the meat and leave 30 seconds to give it time to register, then take it out—it does not roast with the meat. The advantage here, besides accuracy, is that you can test several areas of the meat, since all do not register the same; this is particularly true of legs of lamb, where the circumference varies from one part to another.

Roasting Methods and Roasting Times:

There is certainly more than one way to roast beef. Some cooks swear by the slow roasting method, where the meat goes in a preheated 200°F/95°C oven for 1 hour per pound—per-

Short rib ends and backbone, sawed off

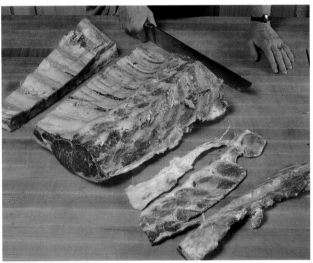

Primal cut

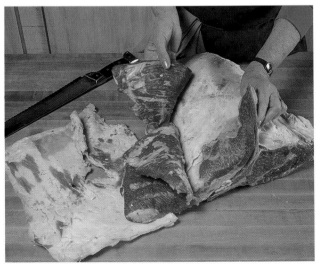

Loin end (above) and shoulder end (below)

fect meat, no loss of weight, and so forth, say they. Other cooks are equally enthusiastic about the Anne Seranne/Craig Claiborne system, whereby you have your ready-to-roast ribs of beef at room temperature and place the meat in a preheated 500°F/260°C oven for exactly 15 minutes per rib; you then turn off the oven and never open its door for 2 hours or even 3 or 4 hours—crunchy brown outside and beautifully rare inside.

As for myself, I like to feel in complete control of my roast of beef, and find that an even 325°F/170°C works well for me with large roasts of three ribs or more. For smaller pieces, which might not brown sufficiently in their shorter roasting times, I sear them first at 450°F/230°C for 15 minutes, then reduce the thermostat to 325°F/170°C for the rest of the roasting, periodically checking the internal temperature with a meat thermometer well before the end of the estimated time. As soon as the instrument registers 105°F/41°C, I check every 5 minutes or so since the temperature can go up rapidly from then on. Here is the meat roasting chart that I use:

Chart for Roast Ribs of Beef

Choice-graded roasts will usually be a little lighter in weight and take a little less time per pound to roast than Prime ribs. In addition, the particular way your market trims its roast determines its total weight, such as how much or little fat is left on, how close to the eye—the main muscle of meat—the ribs have been sawed off, how much of the backbone has been removed, and how much of the cap meat remains on the roast. I calculate 13 minutes per pound (or 450 grams) for rare-roasted, fully trimmed Prime ribs, and about 12 for Choice. The following chart gives rib counts and the weights and time estimates I have figured out for roasts of beef, but timing—if your roast weighs less than the rib count shown here—should be based on weight. Any chart, however, is only a guide, and you must rely on your accurate meat thermometer, starting to take temperatures half an hour before the end of the estimated roasting time. As for number of servings, it is safe to count on 2 people per rib of roast beef, which gives generous helpings and perhaps some leftovers.

Rib Count	Approximate Weight	Oven Temperature*	Total Estimated Time	Meat Thermometer Reading (Rare)†
2 ribs	4–5 lb (1¾–2¼ kg)	450–325°F** (230–170°C)	60–70 minutes	120°F/49°C
3 ribs	7–8½ lb (3–3¼ kg)	325°F/170°C	1½–1¾ hours	120°F/49°C
4 ribs	9–10½ lb (4–5 kg)	325°F/170°C	1¾–2¼ hours	120°F/49°C
5 ribs	11–13½ lb (5–6 kg)	325°F/170°C	2¼–2¾ hours	120°F/49°C
6 ribs††	14–16 lb (6¼–7¼ kg)	325°F/170°C	3–3¼ hours	120°F/49°C
7 ribs††	16–18½ lb (7¼–8½ kg)	325°F/170°C	3¼–4 hours	120°F/49°C

*   Be sure your oven thermostat is correct, or your timing will be way off.

**   Sear a 2-rib roast for 15 minutes at the higher temperature, then turn to the lower temperature for the rest of the cooking.

†   Add 2 to 3 minutes more per pound for less-rare beef (125°F/52°C), and medium-rare (130°F/54°C), and 5 to 6 minutes per pound more for medium (140°F/60°C).

††   I do think you are better off with two 3- or 4-rib roasts than a single 6- or 7-rib one simply because those last 2 ribs at the large end are the least desirable; however, there is no denying the grandeur of that one magnificent spread of meat.

Consommé Brunoise

*Consommé garnished with very finely
chopped fresh vegetables*

Homemade consommé is a wonderful treat,
and I shan't go into the making of it since it is
in both *Mastering I* and *J.C.'s Kitchen*.
When I haven't had the time to make my own,
however, I have used some excellent canned
consommés, one of which is a duck bouillon.
Browse among the shelves of your fancy food
store, try out several brands, then stock up on
your favorites for emergencies. (There is no
reason to be a food snob about canned consommés, say I, since one can simmer them
with a little wine or dry white vermouth, some
chopped onions, carrots, celery, and herbs, and
come up with a very respectable brew for the
following recipe.)

For 6 people

The garnish

1/3 cup (¾ dL) each of the following vegetables, very finely and neatly diced into 1/16-
inch (¼-cm) pieces: carrots, onions, celery,
white of leek, white turnips, fresh green beans

2 Tb butter

Salt and pepper

About 2 quarts (2 L) excellently flavored consommé

Several Tb dry Port, Madeira, or sherry

Several Tb minced fresh chervil, parsley,
and/or chives

Reserve the beans. In a covered saucepan,
cook the other vegetables slowly in the butter
until nicely tender but not browned, then season to taste and simmer several minutes in a
cup or so of the consommé. Blanch the beans
in a quart of lightly salted boiling water just
until barely tender, drain, and refresh in cold
water.

🕐 May be completed well in advance to
this point.

Shortly before serving, pour the remaining consommé into the simmered vegetables
and bring to the simmer; add the blanched
beans and taste very carefully for seasoning.
Off heat, stir in driblets of wine to taste. Pour
either into a tureen or into individual soup
cups and decorate with the chopped herbs.

Remarks:

You can simmer rice, tiny pasta, or tapioca in
the soup to give it more body. You can also
finish it off with a poaching of finely diced
fresh tomato pulp, which adds a pretty blush
of color. You are aiming for delicious flavor as
well as colorful effect, and should feel free to
let your fancy roam—and that can include
diced truffles and mushrooms, too.

Melba Toast

Melba toast couldn't be simpler to make if you can just find the right kind of unsliced bread. The best is a nonsweet sandwich loaf, close grained and a day old—a recipe for just such a loaf is in both *Mastering II* and *J.C.'s Kitchen*. Cut the bread into very very thin slices 1/16 inch (¼ cm) thick; either leave slices whole or cut diagonally into triangles. Arrange, in one layer preferably, on one or two pastry sheets and bake slowly in the upper and lower middle levels of a preheated 275°F/140°C oven for about 20 minutes, or until the bread has dried out and is starting to color lightly. Cool on a rack.

🕐 May be done well in advance, and recrisped in the oven before serving. May be refrigerated or frozen.

Standing Rib Roast of Beef

A 5-rib fully trimmed Prime or Choice roast of beef (or a 3- or 4-rib roast, timed according to roasting chart earlier in this chapter)
2 Tb soft butter
2 medium-size carrots, roughly chopped
2 medium-size onions, roughly chopped
2 cups (½ L) excellent beef broth (see directions at end of recipe)
Equipment
A reliable meat thermometer; a low-sided roasting pan (2½ inches or 6½ cm deep); a rack to fit the pan

For accurate timing, particularly if you are doing a 3-rib roast, leave the meat out at room temperature an hour before it is to go into the oven. And, since I always like plenty of leeway, I start my roasting half an hour to an hour ahead of schedule; in other words, I estimate that a 5-rib roast will take 2½ hours, so I start it 3 to 3½ hours before I plan to serve. It is easy to keep it warm, as you will see at the end of the recipe, and I want to be sure I get it done on time.

Therefore, 3 to 3½ hours before serving, have oven preheated to 325°F/170°C and rack placed in lower level. Smear cut ends of beef with the butter and place it fat side up (ribs down) on the rack in the roasting pan. Set in oven, and there is nothing more to do than rapidly baste the cut ends with accumulated fat from the roasting pan every half hour and, about an hour before the end of the roasting time, strew the chopped vegetables into the pan. Then, half an hour later (in this case, after 2 hours of roasting), start checking temperature. When the thermometer reaches 105°F/41°C, watch closely and check every 7 minutes or so, until desired temperature is reached—about 2½ hours in all. The small end will register the highest temperature, and if you want some meat pinky-red rare and the rest very rare, roast to 120°F/49°C. On the other hand, if you want the small end medium rare and the large end pinky red, roast a few minutes more, to 125°F/52°C, and so forth for more doneness. As soon as the temperature has been reached remove the roast from the oven.

● Keeping the roast warm until serving time: If you know your oven is absolutely accurate and that you can keep it at around 115°F/46°C, turn it off, remove roast, leave door open to cool oven for 15 minutes, then set thermostat at 115°F/46°C and return roast to oven. You can safely keep it in the oven for an hour or two, even longer; the meat and its juices, communing together, make for even more delicious eating. Otherwise let the roast cool out of the oven for 15 minutes, then set it over a large kettle of hot but not simmering water; place the top of a covered roaster or a large pan over the beef to keep it warm. Leave meat thermometer in place and check every 15 minutes or so to be sure everything is under control. The temperature will rise some 10°F/5°C at first, then gradually subside; 100°F/38°C is plenty warm enough for serving.

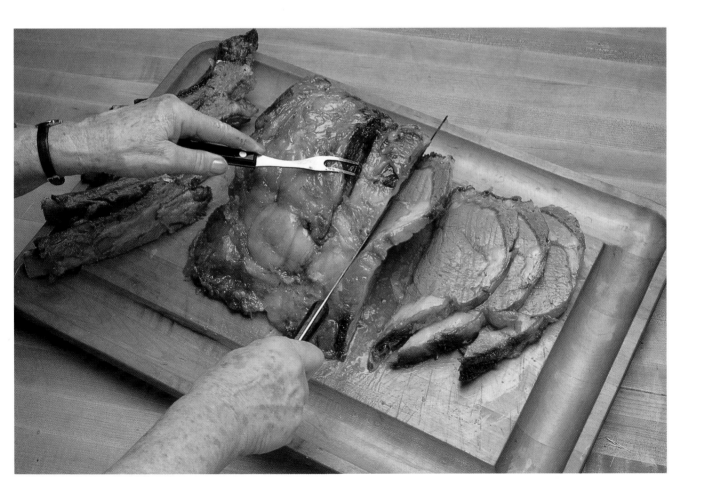

For the sauce or "jus"

Remove beef from roasting pan, pour out accumulated fat, pour in the beef stock, and swish about to dislodge any coagulated roasting juices (there will be little of these if you have roasted to very rare). Pour the liquid and roasting vegetables from the pan into a saucepan and simmer, mashing the vegetables into the liquid. Season carefully to taste, and skim off surface fat. Just before serving, strain into a hot sauce bowl, adding also any juices accumulated from the waiting roast. You should have a tablespoon or so per serving.

To serve

You may wish to bring the roast to the table just as it is, perhaps garnishing the platter with watercress or sprigs of parsley. However, I like to remove the rib bones in the kitchen (another reason for getting the roast done ahead of time); I turn it upside down and cut close against the line of bones, then cut the bones apart. To serve, I set the roast right side up on a big carving board, place the bones at one end, and if there is no enthusiastic carver at the table, I slice a first helping of meat and arrange that at the cut end of the roast. This makes for easy serving, plus the promise of big bones on the plates of those who love them.

Beef Stock:

Brown a pound or more of chopped meaty raw beef bones in a little cooking oil with a chopped onion and carrot, then add a medium-size chopped but unpeeled tomato, 1 cup (¼ L) dry white wine or vermouth, water to cover ingredients by 2 inches (5 cm), and the following, tied in washed cheesecloth: 1 bay leaf, ½ teaspoon thyme, 6 parsley sprigs, and 2 cloves unpeeled garlic. Simmer partially covered for 3 to 4 hours, adding more water if liquid evaporates below level of ingredients. Strain, degrease, and refrigerate or freeze until needed. You will want 1 cup (¼ L) for 6 people; double the amount for 12 to 14.

Timbale of Fresh Corn

For an 8-cup baking dish, serving 8 people

12 or more ears fresh corn (to make about 3 cups or ¾ L cream-style grated corn)

6 eggs

2 to 3 Tb grated onion

1 tsp salt

4 to 5 Tb fresh minced parsley

⅔ cup (1½ dL) lightly pressed down crumbs from crustless nonsweet white bread

⅔ cup (1½ dL) lightly pressed down grated cheese (such as a mixture of Swiss and/or Cheddar or mozzarella)

⅔ cup (1½ dL) heavy cream

6 drops hot pepper sauce (or ⅛ tsp Cayenne pepper)

8 to 10 grinds fresh pepper

Equipment

A corn scraper or grater; a straight-sided 8-cup (2-L) baking dish, such as a charlotte mold 5 to 6 inches (13 to 15 cm) deep, and a larger baking dish in which to set it

Scrape or grate the corn and turn into a measure to be sure you have about 3 cups or ¾ liter. Beat the eggs in a mixing bowl to blend; then add all the rest of the ingredients listed, including the corn.

🕐 Recipe may be completed even a day in advance to this point; cover and refrigerate.

Preheat oven to 350°F/180°C. About 2 hours before serving, butter the 8-cup (2-L) baking dish and line bottom with a round of buttered wax paper. Stir up the corn mixture to blend thoroughly and pour into the dish. Set corn dish in larger dish and pour boiling water around to come two-thirds up the sides of the corn-filled dish. Bake in lower middle level of oven for half an hour, then turn thermostat down to 325°F/170°C. Baking time is around 1¼ to 1½ hours, and water surrounding timbale should almost but never quite bubble; too high heat can make a custard (which this is) grainy. Timbale is done when it has risen almost to fill the mold, the top has cracked open, and a skewer plunged down through the center comes out clean. Let rest 10 minutes or more in turned-off oven, door ajar, before unmolding.

🕐 May be baked an hour or so before serving; the timbale will sink down as it cools, but who would ever know how high it might have been, once it is unmolded?

Brussels Sprouts Tossed in Butter

Here is one method for serving Brussels sprouts that are fresh and bright green. Blanch them until just cooked through, drain and cool them, halve or cut them into thirds, and set aside until just before serving. Then toss them in a big frying pan in hot butter and seasonings, just to heat them through, and serve them forth. A marvelous vegetable when done this way.

For 6 people

Two to three 10-ounce (285-g) packages fine fresh green hard-headed Brussels sprouts

Salt

4 or more Tb butter

Pepper

Equipment

A kettle large enough to hold at least 6 quarts or liters water

Preparing sprouts for cooking

One by one, pull any small or withered leaves off root end of sprouts, shave root close to base of remaining leaves (but not so close that leaves will come loose); with a small knife,

pierce a cross ⅜ inch (1 cm) deep in root ends —to make for fast and even cooking. Throw out any wilted or soft-headed sprouts.

🕐   May be prepared in advance even a day before cooking; cover and refrigerate.

Preliminary cooking—blanching

Fill a large kettle with at least 6 quarts or liters of water, adding 1½ teaspoons salt per quart or liter. Cover and bring to the rapid boil. Meanwhile, wash the sprouts under cold running water. (Old recipes call for soaking sprouts in salted water, presumably to make them disgorge bugs, weevils, ants, and whatnot. I have never found any such fauna in any of my Brussels sprouts, and have therefore never done more than simply wash them rapidly.) When water is boiling, plunge in the sprouts, cover kettle, and as soon as water boils again uncover and boil slowly for 4 or 5 minutes. Sprouts are done when just cooked through but still slightly crunchy and bright green—taste one or two, to verify the cooking. Drain them at once, by holding a colander in the kettle and pouring off the water. Then, with colander still in place, run cold water into the kettle to refresh the sprouts, to set the green color, and to preserve the fresh texture. Drain in a moment or two, then halve the sprouts lengthwise, or cut into thirds, to make them all the same size.

🕐   May be prepared several hours in advance to this point; arrange in a bowl, cover, and refrigerate.

Final cooking

Between courses, and just before serving, melt as much butter as you think sensible and/or decent in a large frying pan, add the sprouts, and toss and turn (shaking and twirling pan by its handle rather than stirring with a spoon). Season to taste with salt and pepper, and sample a sprout or two to be sure they are thoroughly heated through.

Serving

Either turn the sprouts into a hot vegetable dish or surround the preceding unmolded timbale of fresh corn.

Macédoine of Fruits in Champagne

Plan as attractive a mixture of cut-up fruits as you can muster, considering the season of the year. Summer is ideal, of course, with fresh apricots, peaches, cherries, berries, and all the bounties the warm months can offer. December is more of a problem. However, one can still have fresh oranges and grapefruit cut into skinless segments, an occasional strawberry or melon, pineapple, bananas, and grapes to peel and seed. And there are nuts to sliver or chop, and shavings of ginger (either candied or fresh). And, of course, the canned and frozen fruits that can marry with the fresh. Among canned fruits I do like figs in syrup, dark-purple plums, and sometimes mandarin or tangerine segments, as well as the exotic fragrance of a few kumquats, sliced thin and seeded. Frozen blueberries have the charm of deep purple for color, and sometimes whole strawberries are successful. I shall not offer a combination since it is too personal and seasonal a dish, but I do suggest a careful design plan for the arrangement, squeezings of lemon, and sprinklings of kirsch, white rum, or Cognac, if you like such additions. Let the fruits macerate together in their covered serving bowl in the refrigerator for several hours, and taste frequently in case more lemon, or even orange juice, or liqueurs are needed—and you may want to drain off some of the juices before serving. Then, at the table, and just before ladling out, pour some Champagne from the bottle either into the serving bowl or into each dish—that fizzling sudden sparkle of foam transforms a simple collection of cut-up fruits into a dressy *macédoine au Champagne.* Then pour out a glass of the same Champagne for each guest, to accompany the fruit.

Bourbon-soaked Chocolate Truffles

For 12 to 18 pieces

7 ounces (200 g) semisweet baking chocolate
1 ounce (30 g) unsweetened baking chocolate
4 Tb bourbon whiskey or dark Jamaica rum
2 Tb strong coffee
1 stick (4 ounces or 115 g) unsalted butter, cut into 1-inch (2-cm) pieces
6 ounces (180 g) best-quality gingersnaps (to make ¾ cup or 1¾ dL pulverized)
½ cup (1 dL) unsweetened cocoa powder
¼ cup (½ dL) powdered instant coffee
Equipment
Paper or foil candy cups

The mixture

Break up the two chocolates and place in a small saucepan with the bourbon or rum and the liquid coffee. Cover, set chocolate pan in a larger pan of boiling water, and turn off the heat under it. When chocolate is melted and smooth, in 5 minutes or so, beat in the butter piece by piece (a portable electric mixer is useful here), then the pulverized gingersnaps. Chill for several hours.

Forming the truffles

Mix the cocoa powder with the powdered coffee and spread on a plate. With a soup spoon or teaspoon, depending on the size you wish, dig out gobs of the chocolate mixture and form into rough, roundish, rocklike, trufflelike shapes. Roll in the cocoa and coffee powder, and place in candy or cookie cups. Refrigerate in a covered container until serving time.

🕐   Truffles may be kept under refrigeration for several weeks or frozen.

🕐 *Timing*

Since this menu calls for two dishes that need oven cooking, the beef and the corn timbale, can you manage with only one oven? If it's big enough you can put the corn in with the beef. Since you can roast the beef and keep it warm over hot water, as described in the recipe, you can bake the corn after you remove the beef. But with only one oven, you may wish to substitute another vegetable for the corn timbale, attractive as it is; suggestions for other vegetables are in the following section.

In any case, you have few last-minute jobs. The Brussels sprouts, which have been lightly precooked, are tossed in hot butter between courses while you arrange the beef for serving. The timbale stays warm in its baking dish and is unmolded just before serving, and then you can surround it with the hot sprouts. All you do before dinner is check on your beef, remove its ribs if you wish to do so, and reheat the consommé.

An hour before your guests arrive, the timbale goes into the oven and, if you can control oven temperatures, your roast is done and cooling, to be kept safely at 115° to 120°F (45° to 50°C) until you are ready to serve it.

Two hours before dinner, chill the Champagne, stir the final flavorings into your macédoine of fruits, and let it continue macerating in the refrigerator.

Three to three and a half hours before serving, put the roast in the oven. You have set it out at room temperature an hour beforehand, and the oven has been preheated.

In the morning, prepare the vegetables for the soup, blanch the beans (also for the soup), trim and blanch the sprouts, prepare the timbale, and compose the fruits for the dessert.

If you are making your own consommé, you can do so days in advance—it freezes nicely, as do the chocolate truffles and the simple beef stock for the roasting sauce.

Menu Variations, of a Conservative Sort

The soup: Consommé variations are infinite, as a quick trot through Escoffier or even *J.C.'s Kitchen* will show you. You could change from consommé to clams or oysters, or cold lobster or crab as an appetizer. I'm always partial to fish soup, but that might offend a conservative meat-and-potato palate. Better stick to consommé or shellfish.

The roast: Substitute a rib eye of beef (meaning the roast is boned); a sirloin strip—a fine boneless roast this is, less dramatic than the rib but easy to carve; a well-aged Prime rump roast; or a tenderloin. Try a roast leg of veal, if you can get a large, Prime, pale, and perfect piece—not easy. Or roast leg of lamb, if you have an expert carver to handle it. Saddle of lamb is elegant but needs carving expertise, too. Though a roast loin of pork and fresh ham are delicious, they are never considered as dressy for this kind of occasion, unless you know the tastes of your principal guests.

The vegetables: Instead of fresh corn for the timbale, you could use spinach, broccoli, or cauliflower—but these alternative vegetables should be blanched, chopped, and turned in butter first; grated zucchini should be squeezed dry and sautéed in butter. Cauliflower or zucchini timbale surrounded by fresh peas would be lovely. Sautéed mushrooms could surround a timbale of spinach or broccoli. Rather than using a high molded structure for the timbale, you could bake it in a ring mold and pile the other vegetables in the middle for serving. You could get away from the timbale idea entirely and serve braised lettuce or endive and cleverly cut sautéed potatoes or scalloped potatoes, with something colorful and red, like tomatoes Provençal or baked cherry tomatoes.

The dessert: Serve a homemade sherbet of strawberries, grapefruit, or pear. Or fresh fruits, like a fine ripe pineapple, or melon with grapes, or freshly poached fresh peaches sauced with raspberry purée. With fresh fruit, homemade cookies, like almond tuiles, walnut wafers, or madeleines, would be attractive, and you could omit the bourbon and chocolate truffles.

Leftovers

The consommé: Eat it cold or reheated; use for stock; or freeze. The *brunoise garnish,* if not overcooked, makes a nice hot or cold *macédoine* to garnish a platter.

Roast beef: One advantage of a conservative menu with simple (as opposed to composite) dishes is the fine array of possibilities for leftovers. Perhaps you planned in any case to arrange a beautiful cold beef platter for another party; it could be accompanied by a salad or made into one with potatoes, cherry tomatoes, and hard-boiled eggs on lettuce—a Salade de Boeuf à la Parisienne.

I'd save any well-done roast beef, or the coarser parts surrounding the eye, to dice for a hearty roast beef hash, to grind for shepherd's pie, or to grind and combine with sausage meat in patties.

To reheat slices as is, layer them on a platter, cover with foil, and set in the oven at

375°F/190°C; watch carefully and remove when just warmed through. To reheat in a sauce, try adding mustard and cream to your gravy or to some beef broth, or fresh tomato pulp with garlic and fresh basil or dried thyme; if you add red wine, then season it with tomato paste, bay leaf, and thyme, and reduce it by half, you have a great sauce which, if you add poached beef marrow, becomes à la Borde-laise. Or finish your gravy with savory *pistou* or *pipérade.* (For these two preparations, see *Mastering II.* Detailed descriptions of the previous dishes are in *J.C.'s Kitchen.*)

If you have enough of the fine lean eye section, still very rare, you could slice and combine it with mushrooms, onions, and sour cream for beef Stroganoff, or spread it with mushroom *duxelles* and bake in a pastry case for beef Wellington. Or, to serve cold, try it with drinks, in spiffy canapés (on buttered toast, for instance, with a corner spread with caviar); cut in chunks, with a spicy hot or cold dip; or sliced thin and spread with a horse-radish and cream cheese mixture, rolled, and sliced across. Or line cornet molds with small perfect slices, stuff with a piquant mousse or *macédoine,* coat with aspic, and chill till firm —to decorate a cold main dish.

Brussels sprouts: Even if they have been buttered and heated, they should still be green and crisp. You can simply reheat them, or add them to soup, or, if you have lots, make a timbale by the method in this chapter (allowing more milk) or as suggested in *Mastering I.*

If the sprouts have been blanched but not buttered, you have accomplished the first step in a choice of classic dishes. One group, described in *Mastering I,* includes sprouts braised in butter, with cream, or with chestnuts, or gratinéed à la Mornay, or coated with cheese and browned.

Or have the blanched sprouts cold in salad or with drinks. To be posh, you could hollow them out and pipe in a squirt of ham mousse or some savory mixture.

Corn: Any timbale leftovers can be sliced and eaten cold, or easily turned into a hot soup.

As the ears vary so in yield, you may have extra pulp and milk on hand. If so, try corn chowder, or make skillet corn dowdy, corn flan, or corn crêpes (for directions, see "From Julia Child's Kitchen" in the September 1977 *McCall's)*. Or have corn fritters for breakfast; or combine the pulp with other crunchy bits of vegetables, in puffy eggs fu yung.

The dessert: Any fruit which has been champagne'd should be eaten right up. But if you kept some fruit in reserve, the possibilities (according to the combination you chose) are endless. To keep cut fruit, pack it close in careful layers in a glass bowl, pour over orange juice to cover, shake to make sure there are no unfilled crannies or airholes, cover well, and refrigerate; it keeps 2 or 3 days. Serve as is or drained, in a melon case or ripe papaya cases. Or make a fruit salad, or mold the fruit in aspic (but omit fresh pineapple as it's anti-jelling). Or try a hot fruit curry on steamed rice.

There are lovely compotes, hot or cold, with the fruit juices reduced with wine and cinnamon or flavored ad lib with liqueurs or pure vanilla or almond extract; you can present them baked deep-dish fashion under a meringue or pastry lid. Or make a fruit tart in a rich pastry case. A mixed-fruit sherbet is easy; or fruit can be liquefied for a refreshing punch. And if a few fine sections or specimens remain, glaze them in their own well-reduced syrup to garnish an elegant platter.

Postscript

About beef there is always so much more to learn. Since meat is such a big budget item, the whole subject is well worth study, and here are some books you may find useful. All of them were written not as texts but for the consumer.

Barbara Bloch, with the National Live Stock and Meat Board, *The Meat Board Meat Book.* New York: McGraw-Hill Book Company, 1977.

Merle Ellis, *Cutting-Up in the Kitchen: The Butcher's Guide to Saving Money on Meat and Poultry.* San Francisco: Chronicle Books, 1975.

Merle Ellis, *The Great American Meat Book.* New York: Alfred A. Knopf, 1996.

Travis Moncure Evans and David Greene, *The Meat Book: A Consumer's Guide to Selecting, Buying, Cutting, Storing, Freezing and Carving the Various Cuts.* New York: Charles Scribner's Sons, 1973.

Leon and Stanley Lobel, *All About Meat,* edited by Inez M. Krech. New York: Harcourt Brace Jovanovich, 1975.

Phyllis C. Reynolds, *The Complete Book of Meat.* New York: M. Barrows & Company, 1963.

A savory pie, fresh garden truck: an eclectic menu for good sound appetites

Country Dinner

Menu
For 6 people

Mediterranean Hors d'Oeuvre Platter —
 Sliced Green and Red Peppers in Oil
 and Garlic, Anchovies, HB Eggs,
 Olives, Syrian String Cheese
French Bread, or a Braided Loaf

ℭ

Leek and Rabbit Pie with Buttermilk-
 Herb Biscuit Topping
Snow Peas Tossed in Butter

ℭ

Petits Vacherins —Individual Meringue Cases
 Filled with Ice Cream and Topped with
 Sauced Fruits

ℭ

Suggested wines:
A strong dry white with the hors d'oeuvre,
such as a Mâcon, Châteauneuf, or pinot
blanc; a rather mellow red with the rabbit —
Beaujolais, Châteauneuf, Bordeaux, or
cabernet; Champagne, a sparkling wine, or a
Sauternes with the dessert

The marketing list for this meal looks terribly jumbled, for the menu draws on the very different cuisines of the Mediterranean and the Orient, on down-home American cooking, and on the classical French tradition. Nevertheless, the piquant red-green-gold-black appetizer, the cozy, fragrant rabbit pie, the fresh snow peas, and the delicate dessert make a lovely harmony. Nothing very fancy about it, but it's hard to think of a restaurant where you could order all of these dishes. Restaurants tend to specialize. And most restaurants seem needlessly conservative, lagging far behind the supermarkets' resources, which increase constantly in bounty and variety. The supermarkets, in turn, lag behind seedsmen and gardeners, who prove every day that all sorts of "exotics" can flourish almost anywhere.

Though a good market can, in fact, furnish you with all these ingredients, this menu is designed especially to honor the gardeners who grow their own, sometimes on lots half the size of a tennis court. For very little money, they can eat heavenly food like this all summer long. In all but the hottest weather, they can harvest snow peas for months, by making successive plantings; since they pick their snow peas—ordinary peas too—in the dewy morning and refrigerate them at once, the quality is superlative. (If peas are harvested too old, or if they sit even a few hours in the heat after picking, they taste flat. Either way, their natural sugar has been converted into starch.) As for leeks, while you certainly can buy fine ones, the price is shocking except in the fall. That's when the crop is mature, and commercial growers harvest and sell it all at once. The rest of the year, markets must import their leeks from wherever they're mature at the moment.

But leeks are good at any age, and home gardeners pick them when they please. Peppers are expensive because they don't store well, and since they become more fragile as they ripen, the red or fully ripe ones are relatively scarce.

Like most of the Victorian houses where we live, ours sits on a lot big enough to feed us—if we would only cut down all the big old trees, that is. On our one sunny spot, the top front doorstep, we grow pot herbs, but otherwise our crops are restricted to shade-loving things like lily of the valley and a wisteria vine that reaches out to the sun. So it's a great treat for us to dine out with our gardening friends and enjoy their exquisitely fresh vegetables and fruit. Amazing what ingenuity can do in a city backyard! To save ground space, our friends grow strawberries and cucumbers and tomatoes on trellises, and espalier fruit trees on sunny southern walls. Their ripening melons, groaning with juice, hang heavily in little net hammocks suspended from fence posts. Peppers, so beautiful and bountiful, are grown as ornamental plants on patios. And grapevines flourish on pergolas built over heat-reflecting concrete driveways.

And livestock! A very elderly resident, who grew up across the Common from us, on so-called Tory Row, says that at the turn of the century would-be ten-o'clock scholars like himself were roused daily at dawn by cackles and squawks and cock-a-doodle-doos. No such rustic racket around here nowadays; maybe too many sleepyheads took their troubles to city hall. But we do see an occasional rabbit hutch, and their numbers are growing. Few cities have ordinances prohibiting rabbits, since they have zero nuisance value: no smell, clean habits, no diseases in most climates, and no noise at all.

Living all over the world, wherever the State Department sent us, we got used to rabbit as a staple and a delight. The meat is delicate and fine-textured, pearly pink when raw but all white when cooked, with a flavor something like chicken, but richer and meatier. You can use it in any recipe designed for chicken. It's high in protein, low in fat, and, according to the U.S. Department of Agriculture, no other meat is as nutritious. When we first returned to this country, rabbit was hard to find in markets, but now most of them carry it, usually cut-up and frozen.

It's nice to see city people raising their own for home consumption, as country people always have. In these days of scarcity and high prices, it's worthwhile pondering the fact that "one doe, in one hutch, can produce 70 to 95 lbs. of dressed, edible meat in one year," and that a hutch can be less than a yard square. By the age of 2 to 3 months, a "fryer" rabbit weighs 4 to 5 pounds, more than half that when dressed; by 7 to 9 months, a "roaster" rabbit gives you over 4 pounds of meat. Fryers are more easily found but twice as expensive; it's a mystery to me why market rabbits should cost so much anyway, since they're incredibly cheap and easy to raise. We got these inspiring facts from the American Rabbit Breeders Association, which estimates that about half its members are backyard farmers, raising rabbits for the pot. If you're inspired too, you can write to the association at 1925 South Main Street, Box 426, Bloomington, Illinois 61701, and ask for their free *Beginners Booklet,* enclosing 50 cents for postage, or you can purchase their *Official Guide to Raising Better Rabbits.* And should you wish to go commercial, be advised that Pel-Freez Rabbit Meat, Inc., of Rogers, Arkansas, will set you up in business if you ask for a franchise.

Except, perhaps, for the eggs for our meringue dessert, this really could be called a Backyard, rather than a Country Dinner. Wonderful what you can do right in town, I mused, as I cooked this lovely food. My imagination blazing with possibilities, I wandered out into my own yard seeking what might be devoured. Any stuff is potential foodstuff to a cook. (My friend Chef Cazalis of the fine Restaurant Henri IV in Chartres, hearing once of an elephant that would have to be destroyed, acquired and cooked the trunk . . . 250 servings, he says; delicious too.) Wisteria? I thought; lily of the valley? But my gardening neighbor stayed my hand. "Are you mad?" he inquired. "They're both poisonous."

Preparations and Marketing

Recommended Equipment:
You need a large platter on which to display the hors d'oeuvre.

To brown the rabbit, a large frying pan; to simmer it, a 4-quart (4-L) covered pot or flameproof casserole; to bake the pie, the same pot or a big baking-and-serving dish. Obviously, the wider the baking dish, the more crust. The one we used on TV is of American-made earthenware, with a smoky-blue glaze inside; I think it's a beauty.

For the peas, a wok is nice, but you could use your rabbit-browning frying pan.

For the *vacherins*, you need a pastry bag fitted with a cannelated (toothed) tube whose opening is ⅛ inch (½ cm) in diameter. It's very important to have the right kind of pastry bag; it makes things so much easier. The best one I have run into is of lightweight, waterproof, flexible vinyl, as yet not manufactured here but imported from France. Also 2 or 3 large pastry sheets, preferably nonstick, and a 3-inch (8-cm) circular something for marking them.

Staples to Have on Hand:

Salt
Peppercorns
Sugar, preferably superfine granulated
Flour (3 ½ cups or ⁴/₅ L; 1 pound or 450 g)
Optional: dried rosemary leaves
Optional: fennel seeds
Optional: imported bay leaves
Pure vanilla extract
Optional: soy sauce
Olive oil
Optional: cooking oil
Vegetable shortening
Chicken stock, or chicken and beef bouillon
    (3 cups or ¾ L)
Small black olives ▼
Double-acting baking powder
Baking soda
Cream of tartar
Butter
Chives
Parsley
Onion (1 large)
Garlic (1 head)
Optional: lemon (1 large)

Specific Ingredients for This Menu:

Rabbit (4 ½ to 5 pounds or 2 to 2 ¼ kg), cut
    up ▼
Chunk of bacon (8 ounces or 225 g)
Red or yellow bell peppers (2 or 3) ▼
Green bell peppers (2 or 3) ▼
Anchovies (1 can)
Fresh snow peas (1 ½ to 2 pounds or ¾ to
    1 kg)
Leeks (5 to 6 pounds or 2 ¼ to 2 ¾ kg) ▼
Celery (1 pound or 450 g)
Syrian or Armenian string cheese (one-third to
    one-half of a 1-pound or 450-g package)
Buttermilk (1 ½ cups or 3 ½ dL)
Eggs (6 "large" plus 4 whites)
Fillings and toppings for *vacherins*
Dry white wine or dry white French vermouth
    (2 cups or ½ L)

▶ **Remarks:**
Staples to have on hand
Small black olives: I like the "Nice" type of olive packed in brine, or the small Italian olives, also in brine, both of which are full of flavor. You might also try the imported, dry, oil-packed ones. Taste one, and if it seems too salty, simmer them in water for 10 minutes or so.

Specific ingredients for this menu
Rabbit: for your pie, use the "roaster" size, about 4 ½ pounds (2 kg) dressed weight, if you can find one. The small "fryer" rabbit is twice as expensive and is really too young and tender for stewing; but it can be used if that's all you can buy. If you have frozen rabbit, which comes already cut up, it's best if you allow 2 or 3 days' thawing time, in the refrigerator. Do not soak it. Rabbit meat can absorb up to 25 percent of its own weight of water. *Bell peppers:* the green or immature ones keep better than the red, mature peppers, but in any case I'd use bell peppers within 3 or 4 days of buying or harvesting, because they soften and spot quite rapidly. Refrigerate them, wrapped in plastic. *Leeks:* buy them fresh-looking, with firm green leaves. They keep well for a number of days when stored in a plastic bag in the refrigerator.

Mediterranean Hors d'Oeuvre Platter

Peeled sliced green and red peppers in oil and garlic, anchovies, HB eggs, olives, Syrian string cheese

For 6 people

2 or 3 green bell peppers
2 or 3 red bell peppers (and/or yellow peppers)
Salt and freshly ground pepper
2 or 3 cloves garlic
Olive oil
Syrian (or Armenian) string cheese
3 hard-boiled eggs
1 can anchovies packed in olive oil
A handful or so of small black olives

The peppers

Place the peppers on a piece of foil in a broiling pan and set them so their surface is 2 inches (5 cm) from a red-hot broiler element. When skins have puffed and darkened on one exposed side—in 2 to 3 minutes—turn with tongs onto another side, and continue until peppers have puffed and darkened all over. At once, while still warm, cut 1 of the peppers in half and drain its juice into a bowl. Scrape seeds from insides, and cut the pepper into finger-width strips—for easier peeling. Pull off the skin—which should come off easily enough if really puffed and darkened. Cut the strips in half, and place in the bowl with the juice. Rapidly continue with the rest of the peppers.

Note: The preceding system works well for me, but there are other pepper peeling methods listed on page 36 that you might try if you are having difficulties.

Peeled red and green peppers make a colorful beginning when cleverly arranged with eggs, olives, anchovies, and string cheese.

Oil and garlic sauce

Place ½ teaspoon or so of salt in a small mortar or bowl, and purée into it the garlic. Mash with a pestle or the end of a wooden spoon to make a perfectly smooth paste, then whisk in several tablespoons of oil. If the pepper slices are swimming in too much of their juice, pour some of it out, then fold the peppers with the garlic and oil.

🕐 Peppers may be sauced several days in advance of serving; cover and refrigerate, but let come to room temperature (to decoagulate the oil) before serving.

The string cheese

The cheese comes in a tightly twisted 1-pound/450-gram hank, as you can see in the photograph. Untwist it, as shown, and cut as many pieces of it as you think you will need into 8-inch (20-cm) lengths—one-third to one-half the package. Pull strands of cheese down the length of each piece—picky work but worth it. Taste several strands, and if cheese seems too salty, rinse in a sieve under cold run-

ning water, drain well, and toss in paper towels to dry. Before serving, you may wish to toss the cheese in a bowl with olive oil and freshly ground pepper.

🕐 Cheese may be strung, but not sauced, in advance; wrap loosely in slightly dampened paper towels, and refrigerate in a plastic bag. Will keep nicely for a day or 2 at least.

Assembling the platter

One idea for assembling the platter is shown on page 25 in the photograph, with one side for red peppers and the other for green; wedges of egg at the two ends, anchovies over peppers, cheese in the middle, and olives (rolled in olive oil) at the sides.

🕐 Platter may be assembled several hours in advance except for the anchovies, which go off in taste if opened more than a few minutes before serving—at least that is so in my experience. Cover platter closely with plastic wrap, and refrigerate, but let come to room temperature before serving so that olive oil will liquefy.

Peppers must be really broiled black for the skin to loosen easily.

Threading string cheese is a labor of love.

Leek and Rabbit Pie

Serving 6 to 8 people

About 5 pounds (2¼ kg) rabbit, cut up

Optional Marinade:

6 Tb light olive oil, or other fresh fine cooking oil

4 cloves garlic, finely minced

1 tsp dried rosemary leaves

2 Tb soy sauce

The strained juice and the zest (yellow part of peel) of 1 large lemon

½ tsp fennel seeds

2 imported bay leaves

Other Ingredients:

An 8-ounce (225-g) chunk of bacon

1 large onion, sliced

Olive oil or cooking oil

5 to 6 pounds (2¼ to 2¾ kg) leeks, to make 6 to 8 cups (1½ to 2 L), julienned

About 1 pound (450 g) celery, to make 2 cups (½ L), julienned

Salt and pepper

Flour

If rabbit was not marinated, add the garlic, rosemary, fennel, and bay as indicated in those directions

2 cups (½ L) dry white wine or dry white French vermouth

About 3 cups (¾ L) brown chicken stock (or chicken and beef bouillon)

Beurre manié (4 Tb soft butter blended to a paste with 4 Tb flour)

Biscuit Crust:

3 cups (430 g) all-purpose flour (measure by dipping dry-measure cup into flour container and sweeping off excess)

2 tsp salt

4 tsp double-acting baking powder

1 tsp baking soda

8 Tb (½ cup or 1 dL) chilled vegetable shortening

4 Tb fresh minced chives, or 2 Tb freeze-dried

Hiding under this savory biscuit topping is a leek and rabbit stew.

4 Tb fresh minced parsley

2 eggs

1½ cups (3½ dL) buttermilk, plus drops more if needed

Egg glaze (1 egg beaten with 1 tsp water and a pinch of salt)

Equipment:

A stainless-steel or glass bowl large enough to hold cut-up rabbit if you are to marinate it; 1 or 2 large frying pans (nonstick recommended), for browning the rabbit; a 4-quart (4-L) flameproof casserole or covered pot for simmering the rabbit; the same casserole or another for final baking; a pastry brush

Optional marinade
6 to 24 hours

If you wish to marinate the rabbit, which will give it a more interesting flavor, beat the listed ingredients together in a bowl large enough to hold the rabbit pieces. Turn the rabbit in the marinade; cover and refrigerate, turning and basting the rabbit several times with the marinade. Before using, scrape marinade off rabbit pieces back into bowl, and reserve.

Preliminaries

Remove and discard the rind, and cut the bacon into *lardons* (sticks 1½ by ¼ inches, or 4 by ¾ cm) and blanch them (drop into a saucepan containing 2 quarts or 2 L water, simmer 5 to 7 minutes, drain, rinse in cold water, and dry). Set aside.

Cook the onion slowly in a small saucepan with 1 tablespoon oil until tender, then raise heat slightly and cook, stirring frequently, until a light mahogany brown—this is to color and flavor your cooking liquid, later. Set aside.

Trim and wash the leeks—cut off and discard root ends, and cut off the green part a finger width or so from where the white begins, where the green is still tender. Slit lengthwise 2 or 3 finger widths from root, give a ½ turn and slit again, as shown. Spread leaves apart as you wash the leeks under cold running water. Cut into 2-inch (5-cm) lengths, and then into julienne (strips ⅛ inch or ½ cm wide). Trim, wash, and cut the celery also into julienne.

❶   All of these preliminaries may be done even a day in advance; cover and refrigerate.

Browning and simmering the rabbit—Rabbit stew

Cook the blanched bacon slowly in a large frying pan filmed with oil, browning it lightly and rendering out its fat; remove bacon to a side dish, leaving fat in pan. Meanwhile, dry the rabbit pieces in paper towels, season lightly with salt and pepper, dredge in flour,

Quarter the leek lengthwise to get at the sand.

Flour the rabbit on a tray to avoid mess.

and shake off excess. Brown the rabbit pieces on all sides (as many as will fit comfortably in one layer) in the bacon fat, and place in the cooking casserole as each is done (add oil to pan if you need it during browning, and regulate heat so fat is always hot but not burning or smoking). Stir the leeks and celery into the frying pan. Toss and turn to blend ingredients; cover and cook slowly 5 to 7 minutes, stirring up once or twice, until softened. Spread them over and around the rabbit pieces, with the browned onions and bacon, and ingredients from the marinade. (If you did not marinate the rabbit, stir in the garlic, rosemary, fennel, and bay.)

Pour in the wine, and enough chicken stock or bouillon barely to cover the rabbit. Bring to the simmer, cover, and simmer slowly until rabbit is tender when several pieces are pierced with the sharp prongs of a kitchen fork. (Older and heavier rabbits may take as much as 1 or even 1½ hours of simmering to cook tender; young ones as little as 30 minutes.)

Arrange the rabbit pieces in a cooking-and-serving casserole. Skim any accumulated fat off surface of cooking liquid, and taste liquid very carefully for seasoning, adding more salt and pepper if needed, more herbs, etc., etc. You should have about 3 cups or ¾ L. Off heat, beat the *beurre manié* into the liquid, and bring to the simmer, stirring with a wire whip. Sauce should be lightly thickened. Pour it (with its vegetables, but without bay leaves) over the rabbit.

🕐 Recipe may be completed to this point even 2 days in advance (and may be served as is—a rabbit stew). If you are not serving or proceeding, let cool, then cover and refrigerate—heat to the simmer before final baking.

Biscuit dough for crust
Place the flour, salt, baking powder, and baking soda in a mixing bowl and cut in the chilled shortening—using 2 knives or a pastry blender—continuing rapidly until fat is broken up into pieces the size of coarse (kosher) salt.

🕐 May be done to this point several hours in advance; cover and refrigerate—liquid is added only the moment before using, because the baking powder starts its action immediately.

Stir the herbs into the flour mixture. Blend the eggs in a large measure, beat in the buttermilk, and mix rapidly into the flour with a rubber spatula, turning and pressing the ingredients together to form a dough. Scoop out onto a lightly floured work surface, and with the floured heels of your hands rapidly knead the dough to give it enough body so that you can pat or roll it out—the less you work it the more tender it will be, but it must have enough body to hold its shape softly.

Food Processor Note: To make the dough in a processor, first blend dry ingredients and chilled shortening briefly with on-off spurts, then, with the processor going, pour in the mixed liquids and blend again in spurts just until dough has massed. Turn out and knead briefly as described.

🕐 Dough must now be used immediately.
Final baking
About 20 minutes at 400°F/205°C
About half an hour before you plan to serve, have the oven preheated and set rack in lower middle level. Then, with the contents of your casserole well heated, place the dough on a lightly floured work surface. Either pat it or roll it rapidly out to a thickness of about ½

Layering the browned rabbit pieces with the cooked leeks

inch (1½ cm), and cut it into the size and shape of your casserole top. Flour dough lightly, fold in half, then unfold over the rabbit, pressing dough lightly against the sides of casserole. (Brush off any excess flour from top of dough.) Paint dough with a coating of egg glaze, and set in oven. Bake for about 20 minutes, or until topping has risen nicely and browned on top.

🕐   May be kept warm for half an hour or so, as long as casserole contents are kept below the simmer so rabbit doesn't overcook.

Serving

Serve right from the casserole, cutting down through the biscuit crust and including a nice piece of it at the side of each serving; baste the rabbit with a good spoonful or 2 of the sauce—and extra sauce and biscuits are nice to have on hand, too, as in the following suggestions.

Use any handy object the same size as the top of your casserole for cutting the dough.

For extra sauce

Either simmer the rabbit in a larger amount of liquid than you need, or make a separate sauce with the same flavorings—chicken stock enriched with a little beef bouillon, and simmered for half an hour with leeks, rosemary, fennel, wine, and garlic; then strain it if you wish, and thicken with *beurre manié* (about 1½ tablespoons each flour and butter per 1 cup or ¼ L liquid). Serve in a gravy bowl.

Buttermilk-Herb Baking Powder Biscuits:

For about 36 biscuits 2 inches (5 cm) in diameter

The same dough you used for the crust makes very nice biscuits, too—although if you are only making biscuits you may wish to cut the recipe in half.

Preheat oven to 450°F/230°C, and set racks in upper and lower middle levels. Make the dough as described in the crust recipe, and after its brief kneading on a floured surface, roll it out ½ inch (1½ cm) thick; use a 2-inch (5-cm) cutter to form the biscuits. Place them on lightly floured pastry sheets, leaving about 1 inch (2½ cm) between the biscuits. Gently knead dough into a ball after each series of cuttings, roll out again, and continue thus until all dough is used.

Bake at once in preheated oven for about 10 to 15 minutes, or until biscuits are nicely puffed and lightly browned on top. Serve as soon as possible, while they are hot and fresh.

🕐   Biscuits may be kept warm, and leftovers may be frozen and reheated, but nothing has quite the taste of biscuits freshly baked.

Plain Buttermilk Baking Powder Biscuits—for Shortcakes:

This same formula, without the herbs, also makes a very fine biscuit, and is particularly recommended for strawberry shortcakes. In this case, you might want to add a tablespoon or so of sugar to the dry ingredients before the buttermilk goes in.

Snow Peas Tossed in Butter

For 6 servings

1 ½ to 2 pounds (¾ to 1 kg) fresh snow peas

About 4 Tb butter

Salt and pepper

Equipment:

A wok is especially useful here, but a large frying pan, preferably nonstick, will do; a long-handled spoon and fork for cooking

To prepare the snow peas for cooking, pull the tips off and down each side to remove strings. Wash rapidly in cold water.

❶   May be prepared hours ahead of cooking; wrap in slightly dampened paper towels and refrigerate in a plastic bag.

Since snow peas cook so rapidly, it is best to do them really at the moment of serving so they will retain their fresh taste, texture, and bright-green color. Melt 2 tablespoons butter in your wok (or frying pan) over high heat; when bubbling, toss in the snow peas. Toss and turn with spoon and fork constantly for several minutes, until the peas turn a bright green. Taste one as a test for doneness—it should be crisply tender. Sprinkle on salt and pepper, toss with another spoonful or so of butter, and turn out onto a warm serving platter.

String snow peas before cooking.

Petits Vacherins

Individual meringue cases

For 10 cases, the 4-piece assembled kind

4 "large" egg whites (½ cup, or 1 dL plus)

¼ tsp cream of tartar

Pinch of salt

⅔ cup (1½ dL) sugar, preferably superfine granulated—to be beaten in

1½ tsp pure vanilla extract

⅓ cup (¾ dL) sugar—to be folded in

Equipment:

Very clean and dry egg-white beating equipment (see page 109 for details); a 12-inch (30-cm) pastry bag with toothed tube opening ⅛ inch (½ cm) in diameter; 2 or 3 large pastry sheets, preferably nonstick, buttered and floured; a 3-inch (8-cm) cutter or any circular marker

❶   The meringues will take about 2 hours to bake, in all, or you can start them in the evening for 1 hour, turn off the oven, and leave them there overnight to finish baking.

Oven Note: Gas ovens are more tricky for meringues than electric ovens—perhaps, I suppose, because the gas surges on and off, coloring the meringues if you are not careful. You may find that 200°F/95°C is best in a gas oven, but that 225°F/110°C is right for an electric one. But you will judge that for yourself after a meringue session or 2— ideally meringues should hardly color at all; at most they should be only a light ivory when baked. They are, actually, not baking; they are only drying out in the oven.

Preliminaries

Prepare the egg-white beating equipment, pastry bag, and pastry sheets. With the cutter, mark circles on the sheets to guide you in forming the meringues. Preheat oven to 200°F/ 95°C—if you have 2 ovens, so much the better.

The egg whites and meringue mixture

Pour the egg whites into the bowl of your electric mixer (or into a stainless-steel or copper beating bowl). If egg whites are chilled, stir

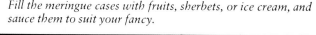
Fill the meringue cases with fruits, sherbets, or ice cream, and sauce them to suit your fancy.

over hot water until barely tepid—they will not mount properly if too cold. Start beating slowly for a minute or so until they are foaming throughout, then beat in the cream of tartar (not needed if you are using copper) and salt. Gradually increase speed to fast and beat until egg whites form soft peaks. Continue beating while sprinkling in the sugar, and keep beating for a minute or more until egg whites are stiff and shining—a spatula drawn through them will leave a distinct path, which remains. Beat in the vanilla, then remove bowl from stand and fold in the remaining sugar by large sprinkles.

❷   Meringue should be used at once.

Forming the vacherins
You may form the *vacherins* all in 1 piece or in 4 pieces, as shown—a bottom and 3 rings that are baked, then glued together with leftover meringue and baked briefly again to set. This latter method produces a so much better-looking meringue in every way that I shall describe it alone—and it takes about the same total time to bake as the 1-piece model.

Form 10 bottom disks in the circle outlines on the baking sheets as shown, then form 30 rings; meringue should be about the thickness of your little finger or less. (Reserve 3 tablespoons meringue for gluing, later.)

Baking
About 1 hour plus 30 to 40 minutes
Set at once in oven or ovens, switching baking sheets from lower to upper racks several times, and watching that the meringues do not color more than a light ivory. Raise or lower oven heat if you think it necessary. Meringues are not done until you can gently push them loose—they will loosen when they have dried out and are ready to come off.

To assemble the cases, spread a thin coating of reserved meringue on the bottom of 1 ring, and set it on a bottom disk; continue with 2 more rings. Assemble all in the same way, and return to oven for another 30 to 40 minutes, until the meringue has dried and glued the pieces of the case together.

❷   Baked meringues may be kept in a warming oven for a day or 2 to prevent them from getting soggy, but the safest place for long storage is the freezer. You may take them directly from the freezer for filling and serving. If meringues are left out on a damp day they will soften and even collapse.

Fillings for Vacherins:
You may fill *vacherins* with fruits or berries; with whipped cream and a topping; with Bavarian cream mixture, which can then be chilled and set; or with ice cream and various fruit toppings as shown here. You can use either vanilla ice cream or a sherbet, and the *vacherins* can go back into the freezer until serving time—the meringue softens after a day or so, but is equally delicious either soft or crisp, at least that is what I think.

A pastry bag makes the neatest forms.

Peach topping

Use fresh peaches, or canned clingstones (more flavorful than freestone). For fresh peaches, slice them and sprinkle with a little sugar and lemon juice and let stand 10 minutes or so, until their juices have rendered out; drain the juices and simmer with a little arrowroot or cornstarch to thicken lightly. Taste carefully for seasoning, adding a few droplets of rum or Cognac if you wish, and fold in the peaches. Use the same system for canned peaches, although they will probably need no sugar—only lemon juice, thickening, and perhaps a few drops of liqueur.

Berry topping

Use the same system described for peaches.

Glue the rings to the base with leftover meringue.

⏱ Timing

You do have some last-minute work for this menu, but not too much. Just before serving the main course, cook the snow peas—a matter of only 2 or 3 minutes. At this time too, if you filled and froze the *vacherins*, put them in the refrigerator so the ice cream will soften a little. If your ice cream is in bulk, however, it may need a good half hour in the refrigerator to soften—unless it is the nonhardening type.

Open the anchovies just before serving the Mediterranean platter.

Set the rabbit pie in the oven when you expect your guests to come; it can wait safely if need be. Baking time is 20 minutes or so, and you must mix and roll the dough right before it goes in the oven; but the dry ingredients can be mixed long beforehand.

Several hours before dinner, you can assemble the hors d'oeuvre platter, and wash, trim, and refrigerate the fresh snow peas. Now's the time to sauce the cheese, if you wish to, and to make the fruit sauces for the *vacherins*.

A day or 2 before the party, you can string the cheese (but not sauce it)—a longish job, so allow for that. At this time, you can make the rabbit stew. If you want to marinate the rabbit pieces, start from 6 to 24 hours earlier.

Several days beforehand, you can peel and sauce the peppers.

The meringues can be made any time and frozen. Or you can keep them for several days in a very dry place; damp weather collapses them.

Menu Variations

Hors d'oeuvre platter: for other ways to use peppers, see pages 36–37. Instead of bread, serve the platter with pita pockets, so guests can make their own sandwiches. If Syrian string cheese is hard to find, try julienned pieces of mozzarella or crumbled feta. Or you could use celeriac instead (see page 43). A somewhat similar hors d'oeuvre is a platter (or several small dishes) of cold, cooked vegetables in a vinaigrette dressing or *à la grecque*: ideal for the gardener-cook who might, in late summer, prefer to offer a leaf-lined basket of home-grown sliced melon.

The main course: cassoulet, the farmer's joy and catchall, would be a hearty substitute for the rabbit pie. You can make this same dish with chicken. Or leave the crust off and serve your rabbit stew over rice, or make a different rabbit stew, like the one with lemon in *J.C.'s Kitchen.* Or make a puff pastry crust. No other vegetable is quite like snow peas, except sugar snap peas with edible pods and full-sized occupants; but green peas or broccoli flowerettes would be nice with the rabbit.

The dessert: instead of topping your ice cream-filled *vacherins* with fresh or canned peaches or berries (see the recipe), you could use chocolate sauce, or shaved chocolate. Or caramel sauce, or simply use frozen raspberries or strawberries puréed in a blender or processor and, in the case of raspberries, strained. Stewed fresh rhubarb is another idea, as is a nut brittle that you have pulverized, or even our old favorite—a spoonful of rum or bourbon poured over the ice cream followed by a generous sprinkle of powdered instant coffee. For a supremely festive look and a delicious prickle on the tongue, you could swathe each little case with spun caramel, or cover each with a caramel cage, as in *J.C.'s Kitchen.* Or set a poached pear or peach in each *vacherin,* and top off with caramel, chocolate, or raspberry sauce. Or make the classic Mont Blanc, and fill each case with a sweetened purée of chestnuts forced through a ricer and surmounted by whipped cream. And so on, and so forth . . .

Leftovers (and Bumper Crops)

Hors d'oeuvre platter: though the anchovies are through for the day, all the other ingredients will keep for several days, well covered, in the refrigerator. For ways to use peppers, see page 36. If unsauced, already-strung string cheese keeps well when properly wrapped (see recipe), and is delightful used like feta (the soft, snowy Greek cheese) in salads and on other vegetable platters. Spare hard-boiled eggs, or egg pieces, can be sieved to top hot vegetables or salads. Or you can stuff cherry tomatoes with egg salad.

The main course: rabbit quickly becomes stringy if overcooked, so, if you want to reheat the stew, keep it below the simmer. The stew can be frozen, or used as a soup (bone and mince the rabbit pieces; add stock). And what about too many rabbits, the classic bumper crop? Australia solved the problem by importing mongooses, which prey on rabbits. More economical would be to find a butcher who rents freezer lockers. *Baked biscuits* can be frozen and reheated, though with some loss of texture. Raw biscuit dough doesn't keep; but see the recipe for ways to use it. *Leeks:* if you bought and cooked extra leeks, use them in a quiche (see *Mastering I*), or a leek and potato soup (*Mastering I, J.C.'s Kitchen*), which you can turn into vichyssoise, or vary with watercress or celery; or serve your vichyssoise *à la russe,* with beets, as in *The French Chef Cookbook.* Extra raw leeks would be delicious braised, and you can serve them sauced and gratinéed (*Mastering I*). Any soup stock is improved by tossing in a leek. And they are delicious cold, *à la grecque. Snow peas:* reheated cooked ones lose their crispness; but extra raw ones will keep a few days wrapped in paper towels and refrigerated in a plastic bag, or invest in Irene Kuo's *The Key to Chinese Cooking* (New York: Alfred A. Knopf, 1977), for all the delicious Chinese ways of cooking them. Or adapt them to a soup designed for ordinary pea pods, in *Mastering II.*

The dessert: extra raw meringue must be used up promptly, and you could change to a large star or rosette tube and make one-squirt meringue kisses, to bake along with the *vacherin* cases. Once it's baked, meringue freezes well. You can even fill cases with ice cream (see recipe) and freeze them that way. But don't let baked meringue stand around in damp weather. Any fresh fruit toppings should be used quickly; they don't freeze well.

Postscript: Pecks of peppers

Why peel peppers, when they're so good with the skins on? They're lovely and crisp raw, in salads; unpeeled, they can be seeded, sliced, and sautéed with onions, or cooked with tomatoes, onions, and bits of ham for a *pipérade,* so delicious with eggs, hot or cold. You can cook and marinate them *à la grecque,* for a cold hors d'oeuvre, or serve a casserole of peppers and eggplant, with plenty of garlic and fresh basil in season. They can help to stuff beef rolls, or zucchini, and with leeks they make a fine soup. Even after publishing pepper recipes in all my previous books, I'm still exploring.

But a peeled pepper is another matter. You have to heat it to get the peel off, so the flesh is slightly cooked; but it has a flavor completely different from what you taste in, say, a baked stuffed pepper. It's very subtle and tender, with an exquisite texture, and the color remains very bright.

Peeling is worthwhile, but it's quite a job. Years after my peeling experiments for *Mastering II,* I did another series which brought me back to my original conclusion, that the broiling method (see the recipe) works best. To get others' views, though, in November 1978 I asked the helpful readers of my *McCall's* column for further suggestions. They offered several. 1) Dip the peppers in boiling water, then pop them into a paper bag for a few minutes. 2) Freeze, then peel. 3) Freeze, then put the frozen peppers in boiling water for 20 to 30

Whatever method you use, skins must really be puffed (left) before you can peel that peck of peppers.

minutes, take off heat, leave for another 5 minutes, and wash with cold water before peeling. 4) Sauté them in a nonstick pan, with or without oil, for 10 to 20 minutes over a very low flame, covered; shake often to prevent sticking. 5) Drop the peppers into hot fat, then into cold water as soon as the skins change color. 6) Use a potato peeler on an untampered-with pepper, cutting it into strips first to make the job easier. 7) Hold a pepper over a gas burner with tongs, turning it to char evenly, then put it in a covered pan.

Covering the peppers after heating them was suggested by several readers, for varying lengths of time, anything from 10 minutes to several hours. I have not myself found it necessary to cover the peppers, since when properly broiled the skin comes off easily.

One suggestion has worked well with the red, mature peppers but less so with the green ones. That is to use a pressure cooker: wait till you see steam, then put on the gauge, bring just to full pressure, and turn off the heat, waiting till the cooker is cool before removing the peppers.

Peppers do vary a great deal, however. Though the broiler method has worked best for me, your peppers may be different; I hope you'll find that one of my correspondents' ideas will help. Just don't give up!

For those who didn't give up, and now find themselves with lovely peeled, sauced, peppers, here are a couple of good ideas for their use, and a recipe for a third. With pasta: either leave the pepper strips whole or chop them into dice, then toss them with hot cooked spaghetti or noodles, adding oil or butter, a good sprinkling of freshly grated Parmesan cheese, and salt and pepper to taste. With cooked leftover rice: make a delicious salad sauced with oil and garlic, and shallots; when you add the peppers, also add some minced parsley, chopped black olives, pine nuts, and what seasonings you fancy after tasting. And here is an excellent sauce to serve with hard-boiled eggs, or boiled fish, potatoes, beef, or chicken, or to use as a dip with cocktail snacks.

Pepper and Anchovy Sauce

For about 1 cup or ¼ L

About ½ cup (1 dL) sauced green or red peppers, page 25

4 to 6 anchovy fillets

1 or more tsp capers

1 or more cloves garlic, puréed

5 Tb or so fragrant olive oil

Salt and pepper

Optional: fresh or dried herbs such as parsley, thyme, oregano, basil

This is easy to make in a blender or processor. Put the peppers in the container of the machine and, if anchovies are packed in oil, add them as is along with some of their oil. If they are salted anchovies, wash them off, split and bone them, and you will probably need no more salt for the sauce. Add the capers and garlic, and purée for several seconds or until smooth. Then begin adding the oil by dribbles until the sauce is the consistency you wish it to be—I like mine quite thick. Taste carefully for seasoning, adding aromatic herbs if you wish them, and parsley for a greenish tinge, if such is your desire.

🕑   Will keep several days, refrigerated in a covered jar.

Pork can be stylish too.

Butterflied Pork for a Party

Menu
For 6 people

Celery Root Rémoulade
French Bread

❧

Butterflied Loin of Pork
Butternut Squash in Ginger and Garlic
Collards, Kale, or Turnip Greens

❧

Gâteau Mont-Saint-Michel —
  A mound of French crêpes layered
  with apples and burnt-almond cream

❧

Suggested wines:
A dry white wine on the light side —Sancerre
or dry riesling —with the first course; a light
red like a Beaujolais or zinfandel with the
pork, or a rosé, or even a sturdy white
Burgundy or chardonnay; a sweet wine with
the dessert, such as Sauternes, or a sparkling
wine

Since fresh pork was "only served at family and bourgeois meals," Escoffier wrote in 1903, in his guide for professional cooks, he "would, therefore, give only a few recipes." Twenty years later, Edouard de Pomiane lamented that "pork is considered to be undistinguished, and at grand dinners one never sees a crisp-skinned pork roast or a fragrant *andouille*" (a hearty pork tripe sausage). Poor piggy, when he's so delicious. The tradition is as old as it is foolish; even the Old Testament, in Leviticus and Deuteronomy, calls him unclean and forbids us to eat him. Pigs do wallow in mud to get cool, but they love a fresh bath and they can be housebroken. (I knew of a very polite pet one, named Ointment.) Thoroughly nice, clean, well-conducted, respectable animals, and I side with open-minded de Pomiane, for whom even the humblest of pork dishes, grilled pigs' feet, was *un plat royal.* Quite right; it is.

Snobberies and shibboleths had no place in the happy world of this great teacher of cooking. Unlike Escoffier, de Pomiane was not a professional chef but a nutritionist, who published the book from which I quote, *Le Code de la Bonne Chère,* under the sponsorship of the Scientific Society of Alimentary Hygiene. It is prefaced with an apology to the great chefs. "Indeed," he says, "unlike them I have not catered to thousands of gourmets. For thirty years I have simply been preparing dinner for myself and my family, experiencing in my kitchen the same scientific and artistic delight I feel in my physiology laboratory, before my painting easel, or at my music stand when we play string quartets." Warmly pro-feminist, he found that the newly liberated, well-educated young women of France scorned cooking as too simple-minded, a hodgepodge of unrelated commonplaces to be learned by rote. Therefore, he taught cooking in a structured, theoretical way, in order to interest minds trained in logic. Yet his books are full of poetic descriptions. Vital, enthusiastic, imaginative, de Pomiane called gastronomy "the complete art" because it appeals to all the senses.

I wish I'd known him, and could ask him over to enjoy this party meal at our table. He would consider this dish to be unusual and distinguished, as indeed it is. In fact, it seems to me altogether appropriate for a state banquet. The only reason de Pomiane could find for the unposhness of pork was that it could be so filling as to blunt the diners' appetites for the courses to follow; but on a present-day menu, this argument doesn't apply at all. Certainly butterflying, roasting, and a final quick broil give this pork a sumptuous quality. The lean, even slices have a close grain like velvet, and carving takes only seconds. The herbal marinade accents a certain undertone in the flavor of fine pork, a subtle taste that is often lost if you accompany pork with applesauce or sauerkraut. And butterflied, it cooks in half the

time of a bone-in roast. People are mistaken, by the way, if they think pork has to be cooked to bath-towel consistency in order to be safe. *Trichinae* — rarely found nowadays — are destroyed at 137°F/58°C, when the meat is rare. At 160°F/71°C, the meat has lost its pinkness and is an appetizing ivory color, and still full of juices.

The roast is prefaced by an hors d'oeuvre that is commonplace in Europe but less known here. Celery root — alias celeriac, knob celery, turnip-rooted celery, and in French *céleri-rave* — is simply a variety of celery that is grown for its great bulbous bottom rather than for its stalks. It's said to be easy to grow, and it keeps well through the winter after harvesting in fall. You can braise it in meat stock or chicken stock, or shred it and sauté it slowly in butter, or boil it and mash it with potatoes, or use it in soup for its intense celery flavor, but I think it is at its finest raw, cut into fine strands, and served up in a mustard dressing. (Most restaurants call it a *rémoulade* sauce, so I do; but a real *rémoulade*, a mustardy mayonnaise with capers and chopped pickles, would be too heavy and oily in this case.)

The squash and greens are for beauty as well as flavor. I'm fond of the sturdy greens, with a taste slightly more bitter than spinach, to offset the pork's suavity, and ginger seems to give winter squash more character, besides complementing the pork.

We'll have our apples after, not with, the pork; if the freezer is stocked with crêpes, a plumply layered gâteau is quick to make: a charming dessert, flavored with burnt-almond cream. To caramelize the exterior, I use my nephews' favorite kitchen implement, my indispensable blowtorch. De Pomiane, who learned to cook on a Bunsen burner, would have loved to play too.

Preparations and Marketing

Recommended Equipment:
To julienne the celery root, you really need a machine of some kind because it must be cut very thin. Some processors have disks with holes just the right size to produce strips the thickness of a rawhide shoelace. I find my little French rotary cutter, which comes with several disks, does a perfect job (see illustration, page 43).

Check that you have a broiling pan, or shallow roasting pan, large enough to hold your big flat cut of pork. And if you haven't one already, I urge you to buy an instant, or microwave-type, meat thermometer—you'll have lots of use for it.

A nonstick frying pan with an 8-inch (20-cm) bottom diameter is needed for the crêpes; and be sure the inner surface of your baking-and-serving dish is that size or larger.

Staples to Have on Hand:

Table salt
Coarse or kosher salt
White and black peppercorns
Dried rosemary leaves
Dried thyme
Powdered allspice
Dijon-type prepared mustard
Pure almond extract
Pure vanilla extract
Olive oil
Optional: salad oil
Flour (preferably Wondra or instant-blending
    type)
Milk
Optional: light cream
Butter (3 sticks; 1 2 ounces or 3 4 0 g)
Eggs (5 "large")
Fresh parsley and/or chives
Lemons (1 or 2)
Dark Jamaica rum
Orange liqueur or Cognac
Sugar

Specific Ingredients for This Menu:

Sirloin half of a pork loin (about 7 pounds or
    3 ¼ kg), bone in ▼
Sour cream
Blanched, toasted, ground almonds (1 ⅓ cups
    or 3 ¼ dL) ▼
Celery root (1 with a 3-inch or 8-cm
    diameter) ▼
Optional accompaniment for celery root:
    green beans, or see Serving Suggestions
    following the recipe for Celery Root
    Rémoulade
Collards, kale, or turnip greens (about 3
    pounds or 1 3 5 0 g) ▼
Yellow butternut squash (about 2 pounds or
    less than 1 kg)
Large apples (1 2) ▼
Garlic (about 7 large cloves)
1 small fresh gingerroot

▶   Remarks:

Pork loin: see the recipe later in the chapter for a picture and a detailed description of the cut you want. You may have to show it to your butcher. With lamb, a "butterfly" means the boned leg, so remind him you don't want leg, you want loin in one piece— the sirloin half of the loin, including the loin strip and tenderloin, the twelfth and thirteenth ribs, and the end of the hipbone. *Almonds:* for blanching, toasting, and grinding, see Appendix, page 1 0 8. Nuts stay freshest when kept in the freezer. *Celery root:* see the picture and information about choosing and storing in the recipe that follows. I'm not talking about the root of ordinary celery, though the taste is similar. *Greens:* collards, kale, turnip greens, mustard greens, and beet greens—any of which will do—are usually more abundant during cool rather than hot weather. When buying any of them, look for firm, fresh, crisp, tender leaves; take a bite out of a few, to be sure the greens are quite tender and sweet, not old, tough, and bitter. Like spinach, they wilt down as they cook, and you will be using only the leafy parts, not the stems. So if they're leggy, you'll need more. *Apples:* buy Golden Delicious, or another variety that keeps its shape during cooking.

The boneless butterflied loin of pork cooks fast and carves easily.

Celery Root Rémoulade

Finely shredded celery root in mustard and sour cream dressing

For 6 people as part of a cold hors d'oeuvre selection

2 to 3 Tb or more Dijon-type prepared mustard

2 to 3 Tb olive oil or salad oil (optional)

4 to 6 Tb or more sour cream

Droplets of milk or thin cream if necessary

Salt and white pepper

1 fine firm celery root about 3 inches (8 cm) in diameter

Equipment:

A medium-sized mixing bowl; a wire whip; a julienne cutter of some sort is really essential

This inexpensive julienne cutter also has slicing and grating blades.

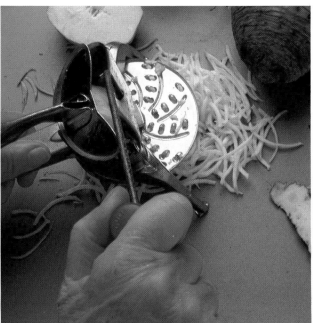

A Note on Choosing and Storing Celery Root: Pick celery roots that are firm and hard all over; big ones are just as tasty as small ones as long as they look and feel whole and healthy. The ideal storage place is a cool dark root cellar, where they will keep throughout the winter and early spring. Those of us without such conveniences should wrap each celery root in a dry paper towel and store the celery roots in a perforated plastic bag (for air circulation) in the refrigerator, where they will keep nicely for a week or more.

When peeled, the flesh of a healthy fresh celery root has a strong and vigorous celery aroma; it is crisp and hard. Its color is creamy white with faint wandering lines of pale tan. As it becomes stale, the flesh darkens and softens.

The Sour Cream and Mustard Dressing: Place 2 tablespoons of mustard in the mixing bowl, then beat in the optional oil and the sour cream; mixture should be quite thick and creamy. If stiff, thin out with droplets of milk or cream. Season well with salt and pepper; sauce should be quite strongly flavored with mustard, since it is the mustard that seems to penetrate and tenderize the celery.

Peeling and shredding the celery root (Because the celery can discolor, you shred it the moment before saucing it.) Peel the celery root, using a short stout sharp knife and cutting just down into the white flesh all around. When you come to the creased portions at the root, slit down into the celery to remove them. At once cut the root into very fine julienne, and toss in the prepared sauce. (If you are doing several celeries, shred and sauce each as you go along, to prevent discoloration.)

🕐 Sauced celery root will keep for 2 to 3 days refrigerated in a covered container.

**Serving Suggestions —
Celery Root Rémoulade Garni:**

You can, of course, serve the sauced celery root as it is, or simply garnished with lettuce leaves or watercress. But I like to dress it up, as we have in this menu, with lightly cooked fresh green beans and sliced tomatoes, seasoned sparingly with oil, lemon, salt, and pepper. However, depending on your menu, you could add quartered hard-boiled eggs and black olives, or even sliced salami or chunks of tuna fish or sardines to make a quite copious first course or main-course luncheon dish.

Julienne of celery root in mustard sauce, garnished with green beans and tomatoes

Pork Talk

Spiced Roast Pork Shoulder:

When I decided to do a menu around pork roast, I thought of a whole shoulder, which I prepared by removing the rind that it came with and slicing off all but a thin layer of fat. Then I put the shoulder in a dry spice marinade for 3 days. It weighed 5½ pounds (2½ kg), so I used 2 tablespoons salt and 1½ teaspoons of my mixed spices (see Appendix, page 109), rubbing salt and spices into the pork all over and packing it pretty airtight in a plastic bag. After its marinade I washed and dried it. Then I roasted it to 160°F/71°C in a 425°F/220°C preheated oven for 15 minutes to brown, and I finished it off at 350°F/180°C, which took some 2 hours in all. It was delicious, juicy, and tender. I highly recommend it to you for pork chops as well as roasts; it gives pork a particularly succulent character.

Stuffed Pork Loin:

Then I said to myself, why not stuff a loin of pork, thinking it would have flaps like veal or lamb that could enclose a stuffing once the loin had been boned; but it doesn't have that kind of folding flap. Instead I cut crosswise slices from the top almost to the bottom of my boned loin so that each slice would be a serving. I made a delicious mixture of liver pâté, sausage meat, shallots, garlic, thyme, and Cognac, spread it over each slice, tied up the roast, set it in a pan with a sliced carrot and onion, and roasted it 1½ hours to the peak of perfection, as they say in the advertisements. But it didn't taste like pork anymore—it was good, but not porky. And it was tough! Why?

About Pork Quality:

I asked my butcher why my pork was tough, and all he could say was that sometimes pork is tough. It's got to be young enough, he told me, and the color should be pale, almost like veal. Several people I talked to said they'd run into a tough pork chop now and then. So our chief researcher, Marilyn Ambrose, got on the telephone to various authorities, including the National Live Stock and Meat Board people in Chicago. David Stroud, president of the board, writes that the single most important factor in getting tender pork is the age of the animal—it should be under eight to ten months old; their ideal is to have all pork for the retail trade six months old. The second most crucial factor is the psychological state of the pig at the moment of slaughter: if it is worn out from traveling, or shocked, or scared, its endocrine glands begin working furiously and that alters the texture of the flesh. Now, if you have ever wondered why your pork chop was tough, you can tell for sure it came from an old and/or scared pig. But who knows if you can observe these signs at the meat counter?

After clarifying the toughness question somewhat, I got back to the idea of stuffing a loin, and back to the boning of one. It's easy to bone the sirloin half that contains both the tenderloin and the loin and a bit of the hip. Looking at that fine big boneless flat piece of meat, I said to myself, why even stuff it—why not cook it just like that? All spread out, butterflied, and slathered with a bit of a marinade—garlic, rosemary, and oil. We'd done butterflied lamb, so why not pork? And a great idea it is, we found; it cooks in a little over an hour, roasted at first, on the inside side, then turned and browned under the broiler on the fat side. And carving is a breeze: you slice off the tenderloin strip, then slice up the tenderloin and the loin strip, giving you chunks for the tenderloin and neat large slices for the loin. As to flavor, it's some of the best pork I've ever eaten.

Temperature control

As noted, there is no excuse at all for overcooking pork, since *trichinae* are eliminated when the meat is still almost rare. I personally like my pork to be done at around 160°F/71°C, when it is possibly the faintest bit pink but more on the ivory side, and the meat has not lost its juice. The Meat Board recommends 170°F/77°C, as do some other sources. I think it is a question of personal taste, and you should try out various temperatures (over 140°F/60°C!) and make the decision yourself.

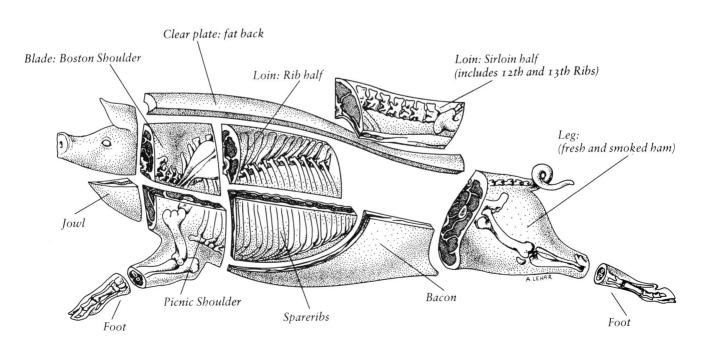

Blade: Boston Shoulder

Clear plate: fat back

Loin: Rib half

Loin: Sirloin half (includes 12th and 13th Ribs)

Leg: (fresh and smoked ham)

Jowl

Picnic Shoulder

Spareribs

Bacon

Foot

Foot

A LEHAR

Butterflied Loin of Pork

Roasted with an herb and garlic marinade

For 6 to 8 people, with leftovers

The sirloin half of a pork loin (about 7 pounds or 3¼ kg, bone in)

1 or more tsp coarse salt

For the Marinade:

2 or 3 large cloves garlic

2 tsp salt

½ tsp each dried rosemary leaves and thyme

⅛ tsp powdered allspice

About 3 Tb olive oil

Equipment

3 skewers about 9 inches (23 cm) long (useful); a roasting or broiling pan large enough to hold meat easily and, if you wish, the bones too; an instant meat thermometer (recommended)

Butterflying the pork loin

The full sirloin half of the pork loin includes the twelfth and thirteenth ribs at the small end, the end of the hipbone at the large end, the loin strip (the large eye of meat on one side of the central bone) and the pork tenderloin, the long conical strip that is small at the rib end and large at the hip end of the loin (illustrated on page 45). To bone, cut down the length of the backbone on the tenderloin side, starting at the small end, scraping always against the bone and not against the flesh. The bone is shaped like a T; the flat top is the fusion of vertebrae that form the backbone, and their fat prongs go down into the flesh, separating the tenderloin from the loin strip.

When you come to the large end, you will have to cut around the hipbone (the only slightly complicated part of the job); then cut around the fat prongs, going up under the T and around it, to separate bone from flesh. Spread out the meat, flesh side up, and cut out any interior fat. Turn it over, and slice off all but a ¼-inch (¾-cm) layer of fat—or more, if you wish, but the fat, which will be slashed and salted near the end of cooking, makes a decorative top.

Cut down length of backbone on the tenderloin side.

Cutting around the hipbone

Cut around the prongs and up, to release backbone.

Marinating the pork

30 minutes to 24 hours

Peel the garlic cloves and purée with the salt. Grind the rosemary leaves, using a small mortar and pestle or small bowl and the handle end of a wooden spoon; add the thyme, allspice, and puréed garlic, then stir in the oil.

Spread out the pork, fat side down, and paint the flesh side with the marinade. Skewer the meat flat, if you wish, and place the pork, fat side down, in an oiled roasting pan.

🕐 Pork may be prepared to this point a day in advance; wrap and refrigerate.

Preliminary roasting

About 1 hour at 375°F/190°C

Preheat oven in time for roasting, then set meat in upper third level. Roast the pork (and the bones too, if you wish), basting with accumulated juices in pan, for about an hour, or to a meat thermometer reading of 140°F/60°C. Remove from oven. (Bones will need 15 to 20 minutes more.)

🕐 Preliminary roasting may be completed an hour before serving; set at room temperature, and cover with an upside-down bowl.

Final browning

About 10 minutes if done immediately

Pork is now to be turned over and browned on its fat side; either place it on another pan or scrape juices out of roasting pan into a saucepan. Turn pork fat side up.

Preheat broiler to very hot. Meanwhile, with a sharp knife cut crosswise slashes ¼ inch (¾ cm) apart down the length of the pork, and sprinkle with a thin layer of coarse salt. Place meat so its surface is 3 inches (8 cm) from heat source, to let it brown nicely and finish cooking. Meat is done (to my taste, at least) at an internal temperature of 160°F/71°C—when it is still juicy. It is a shame to overcook pork! (See notes on that subject earlier in the chapter.)

🕐 The pork may be kept warm for half an hour or more in a warming oven at 120°F/49°C.

Carving and serving

To carve, cut off the tenderloin strip, going the length of the loin. Carve it into as many crosswise nuggets as you have guests, and pile at one end of your platter. Then cut the loin strip into crosswise slices. Skim fat off roasting juices, and spoon a little over the meat; pour the rest into a hot sauce bowl and moisten each serving with a spoonful. (The bones make nice finger food for tomorrow's lunch.)

Herb and garlic marinade enhances flavor.

Score the fat side before final broiling.

Separate the tenderloin (left) from loin before carving.

Butternut Squash in Ginger and Garlic

For 6 to 8 servings

A yellow butternut squash (or other winter squash) of about 2 pounds (under 1 kg)

½ tsp salt

2 to 3 Tb butter (optional)

4 or more Tb meat juices (optional)

2 Tb each finely minced fresh ginger and garlic

More salt, and pepper

2 to 3 Tb fresh minced parsley and/or chives

Equipment:

A good vegetable peeler; a stout soup spoon; a vegetable steamer (optional)

Butternut squash

Preparing the squash

Cut the squash in half lengthwise; scrape out the seeds and strings, digging in hard and close to the flesh. Remove outer skin with a vegetable peeler, going over the squash several times to expose the deep-yellow flesh. Cut the squash into strips, and the strips into thumbnail-sized dice. You will have about 5 cups (1 ¼ L).

🕐   May be prepared ahead; cover and refrigerate.

Cooking the squash

You may steam the squash, if you wish, simply by putting it into a vegetable steamer set in a covered saucepan over an inch or so (3 to 4 cm) boiling water. Or you may boil it in a covered saucepan—my preferred method—as follows. Pour in enough water almost to cover the squash, add the salt and, if you wish, 1 tablespoon butter; cover and boil slowly for about 10 minutes, or until squash is just tender—do not overcook.

Whether you have steamed or boiled the squash, drain the cooking water into another saucepan and boil it down rapidly with the optional meat juices and, if you wish, 2 more tablespoons butter, plus the finely minced ginger and minced garlic. When well reduced and liquid is almost syrupy, pour it over the squash. Toss with the liquid and correct seasoning.

🕐   May be cooked in advance. Reheat the squash (or set over a pan of boiling water to reheat or keep hot). Just before serving, shake and swirl pan by its handle to toss the squash with the herbs.

Variations with Rutabaga and Turnips:

Use the same method with rutabaga or white turnips, which also go beautifully with pork.

Collards, Kale, or Turnip Greens

As well as mustard greens and beet greens—whichever you decide to serve, they all cook the same way

How much to buy?

You'll have to judge by eye, remembering that greens, like spinach, wilt down considerably as they cook, and you will be using only the leafy parts, not the stems. A 10-ounce (285-g) bunch or package of trimmed greens should serve 2 people, but if they are leggy or long stemmed—?

Trimming the greens

So that the greens will cook quickly and retain their bright-green color, you should remove all parts of the stems, going up into the leaves, where stems may be tough and woody. Discard any tough or withered leaves. Wash in several changes of cold water, drain in a colander, and if leaves are large, cut into chiffonade (thin strips).

Cooking

Heat a tablespoon or 2 of butter or oil in a large stainless-steel or nonstick frying pan or wok. Put in as many greens as will fit; turn and toss with a long-handled spoon and fork over moderately high heat until the greens begin to wilt (remove and add a second batch if you couldn't fit them all in the first time, then combine to finish cooking). Season lightly with salt and pepper and, if you are using it, toss in a clove of finely minced garlic (for this menu I would dispense with it because we have enough garlic elsewhere). Continue tossing and turning for several minutes until the greens are as tender as you wish them to be—you may have to add a few tablespoons of water, cover the pan, and steam them for a few minutes to complete the cooking; then uncover the pan and let the liquid evaporate. You may wish to toss them with a tablespoon or 2 of butter just before serving.

🕐 Greens may be cooked somewhat in advance; set aside uncovered. Toss for a moment over moderately high heat before serving.

Collards, kale, and mustard greens

Tear green leaves off tough stems.

Gâteau Mont-Saint-Michel

A mound of French crêpes layered with apples and burnt-almond cream

Here is a delicious, dramatic, and very easily assembled dessert, once you have your crêpes—which can be waiting for you in your freezer. And you can make a gâteau of as many crêpe layers as you wish. The one suggested here will easily serve 8 people, perhaps more, depending on waistlines and appetites. It calls for a burnt-almond cream. And why is it called *burnt* almond? Nobody knows. Why is black butter sauce called black when it is only brown?

Gâteau Mont-Saint-Michel

For 8 people

Batter for 8 eight-inch (20-cm) dessert crêpes:

¾ cup (1 ¾ dL) each milk and water

1 "large" egg

2 egg yolks

1 Tb sugar

⅛ tsp salt

3 Tb orange liqueur, rum, or Cognac

1 cup (¼ L) flour, preferably Wondra or instant-blending (measure by dipping dry-measure cup into flour container and sweeping off excess)

5 Tb melted butter

The Burnt-Almond Cream:

⅔ cup (1 ½ dL) sugar

1 stick (115 g) unsalted butter, preferably at room temperature

2 "large" eggs

1 ⅓ cups (3 ¼ dL) ground blanched and toasted almonds (see Appendix, page 108)

½ tsp pure almond extract

½ tsp pure vanilla extract

3 Tb dark Jamaica rum

Pinch of salt

The Apples:

About 12 large fine apples that will keep their shape while cooking, such as Golden Delicious

Juice of 1 or 2 lemons

Sugar, as needed

Melted butter, as needed

Equipment:

A nonstick frying pan with an 8-inch (20-cm) bottom diameter, approximately (for the crêpes); a baking-and-serving platter of a size to hold the crêpes when mounded; a jelly-roll pan or roasting pan for the apples

The crêpes

Turn to the Appendix, page 108, for directions on how to cook, stack, and store or freeze crêpes. You will need at least 4, probably 6.

The burnt-almond cream

Beat all ingredients together in a bowl with a whip or beater, or in a food processor. If made ahead, stir over warm water to loosen, for easy spreading, before mounding the crêpes.

The apples

Quarter, core, and peel the apples, and spread in a buttered jelly-roll or roasting pan, tossing with as much lemon juice, sugar, and melted butter as you think appropriate. Bake for 30 minutes or so in a 400°F/205°C oven, tossing up several times, until tender.

🕐 Crêpes may be made weeks in advance and stored in the freezer, as may the burnt-almond cream; the apples may be baked a day or 2 in advance, cooled, covered, and stored in the refrigerator.

Assembling the gâteau

Brush the inside of the baking-and-serving platter with a film of butter and lay a crêpe, best side up, in the center. Cover with a layer of apples, then several spoonfuls of almond cream, then a crêpe, pressing down on its center to spread apples out to the edge and to prevent the whole structure from humping in the middle as layers build up. Continue in layers until you have used all but a layer's worth of apples; end with the apples. Sprinkle lightly with melted butter and sugar.

🕐 May be assembled even a day in advance; cover and refrigerate.

Build up layers of crêpes, apples, and burnt-almond cream.

Baking and serving

About 30 minutes at 375°F/190°C

Bake in middle level of preheated oven until bubbling hot and apple topping has browned nicely. If it has not browned, set it under a moderately hot broiler for a moment, or use the professional pastry chef's blowtorch, directing the flame all over the top to caramelize the sugar. Serve hot, warm, or tepid.

🕐 May be kept warm for an hour or so covered on an electric hot tray, or in a warming oven.

Variation—
Giant Flip-Flop Apple Crêpe:

When you have only 2 or 3 people to serve, make them a giant flip-flop crêpe, which you can flame at the table, if you wish. Make the crêpe batter with just 1 egg, no extra yolks, and half the rest of the ingredients. Dice 2 or 3 apples that you have quartered, peeled, and cored, and sauté with butter, sugar, and a spoonful or 2 of rum or bourbon and perhaps a sprinkling of cinnamon—letting the apples caramelize a little in the pan. Choose a large nonstick pan, brush with butter, and set over high heat. When very hot, pour in a thin layer of batter, let it settle for a moment, then spread on the apples; spoon a layer of batter over the top, and cover the pan. When top of batter has set, in 2 to 3 minutes, it is time to brown it. Either turn by flipping it over in the pan and browning over high heat; or sprinkle lightly with melted butter and sugar, and set pan under the broiler, watching constantly, until crêpe browns lightly, in a minute or 2.

Slide it out onto a hot platter, and if you wish to flame the crêpe at the table, sprinkle with a little more sugar, pour over it several spoonfuls of hot Cognac or bourbon or rum, and ignite with a lighted match. Then spoon the flaming liquid over the crêpe for a few seconds while the flames die down. Serve in wedges.

🕐 The cooked crêpe can wait, but it all goes so quickly that I think it best done at the last moment.

🕐 *Timing*

This is what I'd call a mother-in-law dinner: impressive, fresh-tasting, sophisticated food with no last-minute fluster.

In less than 5 minutes, between courses, you can toss the two vegetables in their buttered pots, defat the meat juices, and slice the pork.

Since the pork and the gâteau can safely sit in a warming oven, your only job after the guests arrive is to take the previously arranged hors d'oeuvre platter from refrigerator to table.

Half an hour before serving, brown the pork under the broiler. If you don't have a separate broiler, it's safe to remove the baked gâteau from the oven while the meat browns; it'll keep warm under an inverted bowl. Give the greens a preliminary cooking.

An hour before serving, set the gâteau in the 375°F/190°C oven, along with the pork, which has already been cooking for half an hour. (This gâteau doesn't mind sharing an oven, though a cake or a soufflé would.)

Several hours before dinner, cook the squash, for rewarming later. Do the squash first, and let its juices reduce while washing and trimming the greens. If you're having green beans and sliced tomatoes with the celery root, blanch the former and peel and slice the latter now, arrange your hors d'oeuvre platter, and refrigerate, covered with plastic wrap. Don't put the celery root on the platter till serving time, since the other vegetables would soak up some of its sauce, and you want contrast.

The day before your party, bone the pork and refrigerate in its marinade. You can assemble the gâteau now, and refrigerate till baking time. The apples can be baked a day before this, and refrigerated.

Two days ahead, you can shred and sauce the celery root, which actually improves by keeping.

Any time at all, you can make and freeze the crêpes and the burnt-almond cream.

Menu Variations

Celery root: it's unique, and can only be had in the fall or winter months. What would be nice before the pork? Nothing rich like a pâté or quiche. What about a cold soup or hot consommé sparked with a dash of Port wine?

Butterflied pork: this, too, is unique. Pork cooked by traditional methods (lots of recipes in *Mastering I*) tastes nothing like it. Butterflied lamb is delicious, but, again, quite different, and I think I'd want other vegetables with it.

Winter squash: you could use root vegetables as a substitute, like rutabagas or turnips or salsify (oyster plant). Or new potatoes.

Greens: you could use young beet or mustard greens, or chard (save the delicious chard stems for another dish), or spinach, broccoli, or Brussels sprouts.

Gâteau: like King Solomon when he was sick of love, I comfort me with apples all the time; all my books have apple desserts. I wonder how this gâteau would be with pears?

Leftovers

Celery root: since it keeps very well in its mustard sauce, do make extra, and see the recipe for suggested garnishes.

Butterflied pork: it's excellent cold. Rewarmed, I think it's best in a sauce, either diced or ground, or perhaps sliced, but in any case heated *with* the sauce. If you just have scraps,

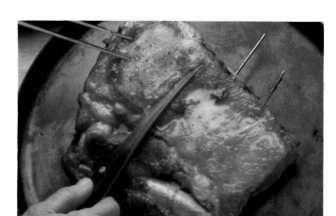

they can be hashed or dropped into a soup (wonderful in a hearty bean or split pea soup).

Vegetables: Fine added to soup.

Gâteau: you can reheat it, or you can serve it cold. If you made extra crêpes, freeze them, and the same for almond cream, which you can use like hard sauce on hot desserts, as stuffing for a *pithiviers*, or in your own improvisations. It's a versatile kitchen staple.

Postscript: Learning to cook

As a penniless student at the Sorbonne, Edouard de Pomiane used to cook his own lunch in the laboratory, presumably over a Bunsen burner. Eventually he was caught in the act by his mentor and professor, who, instead of reprimanding him, appeared the next day with two chops and "a superb *gâteau feuilleté*" and asked de Pomiane to cook for two. De Pomiane describes the event:

"Where did you learn cooking?" he asked me.

"In your physiology course," I replied.

It was the truth. From his lucid teaching, I had learned what meat is. . . . I had heard him speak of the coagulation of albuminoids and the caramelization of sugars. . . .

"Why then," Dastre told me, "Brillat-Savarin was wrong in saying that 'one may become a cook but one has to be born a *rôtisseur*.' Anyone will know how to grill meat if he takes the trouble to think about what's going on during the grilling."

Think what you're doing is indeed a golden rule. Think not just about the why but about the how, for you can save a great deal of time by mastering routine processes. I was surprised the other day to find that one of the *J.C. & Co.* team, who has cooked for twenty years, had never really learned to chop parsley. She was holding the knife wrong, and, though the parsley did get chopped, it took ten minutes.

On the other hand, I didn't know until she told me that chopped parsley freezes perfectly. I'd just assumed it didn't, or just hadn't

tried it . . . like the butterflied pork in this chapter. Butterflying is for leg of lamb, I thought, and thought no more. *Don't take things for granted.* Keep searching for better techniques, new applications, new ways of combining flavors. *Try things out.* One's imagination can play one false: the only real test is to taste.

Try things twice, and yet once more. "It has worked this way for me" is a valid judgment; you have to trust yourself and your experience. But be willing to test again and again — you may have done something just a shade differently the other time, and a little change in measurements or techniques can sometimes make a real difference. De Pomiane, in his classes, taught cooking as an exact and orderly science, but as an experimental science, too. In a laboratory, in theory if not always in practice, the constant factors can be controlled, so you can get a fair look at the variable; but that's not always true in a kitchen. As an example, it took me 29 trials to solve the mystery of a fresh strawberry soufflé. It worked fine that time, but it was far too fragile. The strawberries too often sank to the bottom of the baking dish, and finally I had to abandon the original recipe altogether and develop a quite different technique for keeping the strawberries suspended where they belonged.

Time yourself. Find out not only how long it takes you to accomplish a whole recipe, but also how much time you need to slice a pound of mushrooms or peel six tomatoes. The result of such self-awareness is order, efficiency, and composure. Some menus, especially those with several last-minute jobs, demand it of you.

Eat out. Drink good wine. It doesn't have to be often, but your palate becomes dulled, if you go too long without stimulus or without quality. That's when an otherwise excellent cook will begin to overseason.

Respect your work. Noncooks think it's silly to invest two hours' work in two minutes' enjoyment; but if cooking is evanescent, well, so is the ballet. As de Pomiane put it, "Gastronomy is an art, because in addressing our senses it refines them, and because it evolves, in turn, as a consequence of their refinement."

*For an intimate celebration —beauty, luxury,
excellence, and ease*

Rack of Lamb for a Very Special Occasion

Before we go on to splurge on rack of lamb, that acme of expensive chic, please note that the back porch of this chapter, the Postscript, is comfortably occupied by two cozy, homey recipes for budget cuts of lamb. But tonight we're celebrating with all the stops out. Our guests are great travelers and restaurant connoisseurs, and in fact our first thought was to take them out for the kind of dinner they most appreciate. There are fine new restaurants around here, often run by young women chefs (our chefs Marian and Sara, for example), which have raised local standards to a much higher level of sophistication than we used to see. We *could* go out —but afterward, where would we install ourselves, as the French say, for the second half of the affectionate reunion that we all expect to go on until midnight?

And think of the price! Rack of lamb is not cheap at home, but it's half what it would be in a restaurant. And the nice thing is, it involves very little effort or last-minute preparation. (We've noticed about meat that, the fancier the cut, the less trouble for the cook.)

So, home it is, and our easy menu gives us plenty of time to gussy up the place for that soigné look one enjoys in a top restaurant. Pat Pratt of the *J.C. & Co.* team folded our napkins into the fleur-de-lys shape she learned from her Danish grandmother. Tonight, we've tucked the crisp white flower-forms into big goblets—clear ones, not tinted, so we can enjoy the color of the wine. When we choose things for the table, our first thought is whether they make the food look appetizing (as some magnificent china does not), and our second, whether they involve much fuss. The time we'd have to spend polishing silver we'd rather spend cooking.

At this dinner the food itself is so ornamental that it needs only the simplest setting. We left an inch of deliciously edible stem on the hollowed artichoke halves so that, heaped with the gold and pink of shrimp in an eggy vinaigrette, they'd have the air of bounteous little scoops. Interlaced like two Spanish combs, the racks of lamb are sculpturally elegant, yet the serving is not hindered at all. The crisp emerald-green watercress sets off the perfect trim of the slim ribs, and the little golden carrots, gleaming with butter, provide a soft contrast in color and form. For the dessert, we found a bowl with a deeply scalloped rim to support the fragile cookie cornucopias around the rosy heap of strawberries; if one were lucky enough to own a Monteith, one of those punch bowls with crenelated sides that hold glasses, a truly splendorous effect could be achieved here.

The nicest food of all—I've said it before and will doubtless say again—gratifies all the senses at once, not just taste and scent, but sight, and even touch. All three of these courses tempt one to use fingers: the artichoke leaves, the last nibbly bits on the lamb ribs, the plump strawberries you take by the stem and dip into the cream-filled cornets. Whether the crisp dry crunch of these delicate cookies is more pleasant to feel or to hear, one can hardly say. . . .

"Our cat has a long tail tonight," once remarked Abraham Lincoln to dressy Mrs. Lincoln. Maybe it was Inauguration Night, for which that stout party wore enough purple velvet to drape a hearse, as you can see in the Smithsonian. Well, we're not that ambitious; but here we are with the house looking nice, an impeccable dinner well in train, a joyous reunion to come, and half an hour in hand. What about soaking in a leisurely lemon verbena bath to honor *la vie en rose?*

Preparations and Marketing

Recommended Equipment:
To trim the lamb, you'll need a slicing knife, a paring knife, and possibly a small meat saw. To cook it, foil to protect the bare bones, and a roasting pan; to serve it with the racks interlaced and garnished, a wide platter.

A food processor is useful but not essential for grinding lamb to stuff tomatoes, for slicing onions and potatoes. For grinding nuts for the Plantation Cookies, you could use a knife or a nut chopper. You need a baking dish for the tomatoes, a baking-and-serving dish for the gratin, and a good-sized saucepan for the carrots.

To bake the cookies, you need a wide flexible spatula or a pancake turner. To form them, use metal cookie horns, or make your own out of brown paper (illustrated on page 67). Since baking is brief and precisely timed, a kitchen timer is a must.

I almost forgot cookie sheets. My oven repairman tells me that he often has calls from cookie cookers who complain that their oven thermostats are not working properly. It turns out that the cooks were apt to shove such large cookie sheets into their ovens that the heat could not circulate properly, and naturally the thermostats and the ovens themselves could not function as they should. He advises using a cookie sheet (or a baking sheet for any purpose) that will leave at least 1 inch (2½ cm) of air circulating all around its edges.

Staples to Have on Hand:

Salt
White and black peppercorns
Optional: hot pepper sauce
Granulated sugar
Confectioners sugar
Cream of tartar
Imported bay leaves
Dried thyme
Dried tarragon leaves
Optional: mixed herbs
Dijon-type prepared mustard
Pure vanilla extract
Wine vinegar
Light olive oil or best-quality salad oil
Optional: fresh peanut oil
All-purpose flour
Butter
Eggs (4 "large")
Heavy cream (1 pint or ½ L)
Fresh white nonsweet bread for crumbs
Garlic
Shallots or scallions
Parsley

Lemons (1)
Celery (1 stalk)
Dry white wine or dry white French vermouth
Dark Jamaica rum and kirsch

Specific Ingredients for This Menu:

Cooked shellfish (see recipe); or use raw mush-
   rooms (1½ cups; 12 ounces or 340 g) ▼
Racks of lamb (2, plus meat trimmings from
   them; see buying notes, page 59)
Artichokes (3 large fine)
Carrots (36 to 48 if 2 inches; 12 to 13 if large)
Eggplant (1 firm shiny, about 9 by 5 inches)
Tomatoes (3 large firm ripe)
"Boiling" potatoes (12 to 16 medium)
Onions (8 or 9 large)
Optional: watercress
Strawberries (about 2 quarts or 2 L)
Hazelnuts (¾ cup; 3 ounces or 85 g), shelled
   (also called filberts)
Grated Swiss cheese, or a mixture (1½ cups or
   3½ dL)
Chicken stock (6 to 7 cups or 1½ to 1¾ L)

Some Mournful Remarks on Shellfish:
What filling to choose for the artichokes is a
question of what is best and freshest-tasting in
the market. I am sorry to report my growing
disillusion with frozen shrimp, which, if I buy
them peeled, have a pervasively chemical taste
that seems slightly less pronounced in the frozen shrimp in shell that I find. Canned shrimp
can be mushy, and fresh shrimp are rare indeed. The canned lobster I have sampled has
been unthinkably bad in texture and taste, but
I have tried some acceptable frozen lobster
meat. Canned pasteurized refrigerated crabmeat, though terribly expensive, has been reliable in sauced dishes, but I have suffered some
very poor examples of ordinary canned crab in
the lower price ranges. Some frozen crabmeat
has been excellent—when properly frozen and
stored, and eaten soon—but frozen crab (and
lobster too) must be thawed slowly in the refrigerator for a day or 2 to prevent it from be-
coming watery; I am told this has something
to do with ice crystals that pierce the flesh if
the thawing is too abrupt. If you cannot find
good shrimp, crab, or lobster, switch to scal-
lops, lightly poached in wine, or fresh raw
mushrooms diced and tossed in the sauce.

Artichoke Scoops with Shellfish

*Halved boiled artichokes and shellfish
in egg yolk vinaigrette*

For 6 people as a first course

Egg Yolk Vinaigrette:

½ Tb very finely minced shallots or scallions

½ tsp or more salt

¼ tsp dried tarragon leaves

1 raw egg yolk

1 tsp Dijon-type prepared mustard

1 Tb each lemon juice and wine vinegar

6 Tb light olive oil or best-quality salad oil

Freshly ground pepper

Drops of hot pepper sauce (optional)

Other Ingredients:

About 1½ cups (12 ounces or 340 g) cooked
shellfish meat, or raw mushrooms

Artichoke scoops filled with shellfish

It is easy to scoop out the choke with a teaspoon.

Salt, pepper, oil, lemon juice—as needed

3 large fine boiled or steamed artichokes

The vinaigrette
Mash the shallots or scallions in a small bowl with the salt, then with the tarragon. Beat in the yolk and mustard, then the lemon juice and vinegar. In a small stream, beat in the oil. Season to taste with pepper, hot pepper sauce, and more salt if needed. Sauce should be a pale-yellow cream with a light thickening so that it will film the shellfish but not mask it.

❶ Best made shortly before using. If it separates, shake in a screw-topped jar.

Assembling
Turn the shellfish (or mushrooms) into a bowl, and pick over to remove any possible debris. Fold in the dressing and let sit 10 minutes, folding several times. Taste, and add lemon, oil, and/or seasonings if you feel them necessary. Slice the artichokes in half lengthwise, and scoop out the central core of leaves and the chokes with a teaspoon. Shortly before serving, pile sauced filling into each cavity.

❶ It is best not to sauce the filling too far ahead for fear the sauce might separate. Instead, toss the shellfish with salt, pepper, and drops of lemon juice and oil; cover and refrigerate. Fold in the sauce and assemble 10 minutes before serving.

To Boil or Steam Artichokes the Simplest Way:
First hold each artichoke head under a stream of cold water, spreading the leaves gently apart to give a thorough washing. Slice off ½ inch (1½ cm) from the bottom of the stems, and pull off any small or withered leaves at the base. To boil, drop them into a large kettle of enough boiling salted water to submerge them completely, and boil slowly for 30 to 40 minutes, or until bases of artichokes are tender, and the bottom of a leaf is tender when you pull it through your teeth. To steam them, place in a vegetable rack in a covered kettle with 2 inches (5 cm) of water, and steam 30 to 40 minutes or until tender. Drain the artichokes bottom up, and serve them hot, warm, or tepid—or cold for the preceding recipe.

Buying and Trimming a Rack of Lamb

The rack of lamb is the whole rib chop section from one side of the lamb, going from the tip of the shoulder blade to the beginning of the loin, and comprising ribs number 6 through 12. (The official name for the rack is "lamb rib roast.") Although not as expensive as the saddle, which is the whole loin chop section from both sides of the lamb, the rack is a luxurious cut of exquisitely flavored tender meat. But there is not very much of it: 1 rack will serve only 2 to 3 people.

If you look closely at the photograph of our lamb here, which is indeed a fine specimen, you can see the purple grading stamp on the fat, U.S.D.A. Prime, which is the official federal classification for the very best grade of meat, more often reserved for restaurants than for the retail markets where most of us shop. Choice, the next grade, is very good too, but just not quite as perfect in every category and therefore not quite as expensive.

How to recognize quality in a rack of lamb
Look for the purple grade stamp, which should be left on the meat. The color of the meat should be fresh and deep bright red, with almost a silky sheen to it; the fat should be hard

Left to right: shoulder, rib section (or rack), loin (or saddle), the two legs (or baron). I'm holding a rack.

and creamy white; the eye of the meat—the large, most edible part of it—should be reasonably big and rounded. When you turn the rack over and look on the underside, the bones should be tinged with pink, and slightly rounded—they whiten and flatten with age. The best way to pick fine meat, for most of us, is to find a good meat market and make friends with the head butcher. Butchers are human, and most of them blossom into real friendliness when they find an interested customer who, too, is serious about meat.

To trim a rack of lamb

A rack of lamb is easy to trim, and it is not a bad idea to do it yourself—then you know it will be done right. Besides, you will get all the meat scraps to use, and the bone for making your sauce.

1)Removing backbone. The backbone should be very carefully detached from the tops of the ribs (on the underside or rib side of the rack), in such a way that the eye of the meat, lying right under the backbone, is not disturbed. If you don't have a saw, you can ask the butcher to do this for you, but ask him please to be very careful. When the tops of the ribs are loose, very neatly detach the meat from the under part of the backbone, then detach the backbone from the strip of fat covering the top side of the meat.

2)Trimming rack to expose lower ribs. Cut right down to the rib bones, about halfway from their tip ends to the eye of meat, as shown, cutting straight across, then slicing against ribs and down to rib ends.

3)Trimming excess fat and "cap" meat off the rack. One end of the rack is a little heavier than the other, because there are two layers of meat, with fat, covering the eye of the meat at that end. You want to remove all but a thin covering of fat. Start at the shoulder, or heavier, end.

*4)*Note the eye of the meat. Lift, pull, and cut extra meat and fat layers off—they separate easily—leaving only a thin layer of fat over the whole eye area.

5)Frenching the bone ends. Cut the meat out from between the rib bones, then scrape the bones clean—this is picky work, but worth it if you want the rack to look its luxury price.

6)The trimmed rack. The fully trimmed rack illustrated here weighs less than 1½ pounds (¾ kg) with the fat, the cap meat, and the backbone removed. An untrimmed rack weighs 3½ pounds (1½ kg). However, you do have the backbone to use, and you can also recuperate a handful of usable meat between the fat layers you removed from the top and from between the ribs.

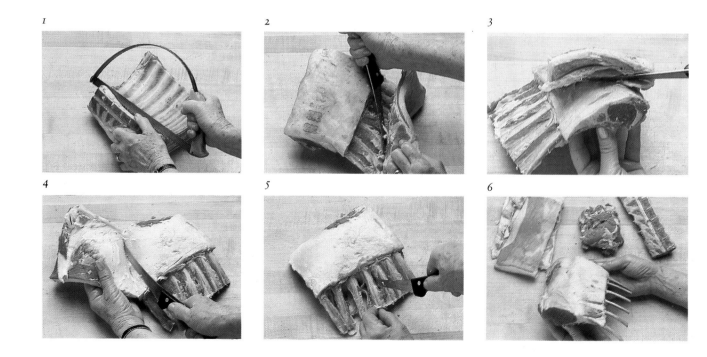

Roast Rack of Lamb

Carré d'agneau

Although the trimmed rack of lamb looks small, it does take about half an hour to roast in the oven. You can make the racks ready to roast well ahead; then, after their first searing, they need no more attention for 15 minutes — which could give you time for your first course. I have suggested a mustard and bread crumb coating here, which browns nicely and furnishes a gentle crunch.

For 6 people

2 racks of lamb, fully trimmed (see preceding directions)

For the Mustard Coating:

1 clove garlic

½ tsp salt

½ tsp dried thyme

2 to 3 Tb prepared Dijon-type mustard

3 to 4 Tb light olive oil or fresh peanut oil

Other Ingredients:

½ cup (1 dL) crumbs from fresh white nonsweet bread

3 to 4 Tb melted butter

A little sauce for the lamb (see directions following recipe)

Watercress leaves or parsley, for garnish

Equipment:

Aluminum foil to cover rib ends; a kitchen timer and an instant (microwave) meat thermometer are useful

Preparing the lamb for the oven

Score the tops of the racks lightly — making shallow crisscross knife slashes in the covering fat. Mash the garlic and salt together in a small bowl, mash in the thyme, then beat in the mustard and the oil. Paint mixture over tops and meaty ends of racks.

Set racks meat side up on an oiled roasting pan, and fold a strip of foil over the rib ends to keep them from scorching.

🕐 May be prepared several hours in advance; cover and refrigerate.

Roasting the racks of lamb

25 to 30 minutes

Preheat oven to 500°F/260°C and set oven rack in upper middle level. The first part of the roasting is to sear the lamb; when oven is ready, put the racks in and set timer for 10 minutes. When time is up, slide out oven rack and rapidly spread a coating of bread crumbs over the top of each rack, and baste with dribbles of melted butter. Turn thermostat down to 400°F/205°C, and roast for 15 minutes more, then begin checking. Lamb is done to a nice rosy rare at 125°F/52°C on an instant meat thermometer — or when the meat, if pressed with your finger, begins to show a slight resistance rather than being squashy like raw meat. (When you have a

After its mustard coating, cover rib ends with foil, and the lamb is ready for the oven.

special, expensive roast like this, it is better to err on the side of rareness, since it is a shame to serve it overdone unless, of course, your guests prefer their lamb that way.)

⏱ Although you are safer serving the lamb soon after it is done—giving it a few minutes before carving for the juices to retreat back into the meat—you can let it wait. Be sure, however, that you set it at a temperature not over 120°F/49°C so it cannot overcook—use a reliable warming oven, or let your roasting oven cool off with the door open and check with an oven thermometer before you put the racks back again. You can also do the preliminary searing, then set the lamb at room temperature and continue the final roasting in half an hour or so. The crucial consideration is that it not overcook. (I made the terrible mistake, once, of setting my beautiful, madly expensive, perfectly

Roast racks of lamb with their crisp mustard and bread crumb coating

roasted ribs of beef in the upper part of a double gas oven combination to wait for half an hour. The lower oven was on, and although the upper oven was off, that lower oven overheated my upper oven and the waiting roast came out well done. Tears of rage, but a lesson learned.)

Serving

The interlaced rib arrangement in the photograph here is attractive for 2 racks of lamb, and carving is easy. You cut down between the ribs on each side, and each guest gets 2 perfectly trimmed chops. Spoon a little sauce around the chops, garnish with watercress or parsley, and the buttered carrots.

A Little Sauce for the Lamb:
About 2 hours' simmering time

There will be little or no juice in the roasting pan because the lamb is cooked rare and no juices escape. But it is nice to have a little sauce to moisten the meat, and you can easily make one—but you will have to plan ahead for it—using the backbones you removed from the racks.

Whack the bones into convenient chunks and brown them in a medium-sized saucepan with 2 tablespoons oil, and a chopped onion and carrot. Sprinkle on 2 tablespoons flour and let brown for several minutes, stirring. Remove from heat and blend in ½ cup (1 dL) or so of dry white wine or vermouth, and 2 cups (½ L) chicken stock. Bring to the simmer, skim off scum for several minutes, then add a small celery stalk, a mashed garlic clove, ½ teaspoon dried thyme, and an imported bay leaf. Cover partially and simmer about 1½ hours, skimming occasionally and adding water if liquid evaporates below ingredients. Strain into another saucepan, degrease, and carefully correct seasoning. You should end up with a cup or so of delicious slightly thickened light-brown sauce that tastes like lamb, and that will complement but not in any way overpower the delicate flavor of your roast.

Buttered Carrots

As a garnish

Your carrots must be delicious to eat, as well as providing color on the platter. Frozen or canned carrots simply will not do because they are, in my experience, mushy, and they certainly lack the flavor of fresh carrots. Baby fresh carrots, however, unless one has them fresh from a neighboring garden, can often be flavorless and textureless, too. Far better in many instances to trim mature fresh carrots, and have them taste as they should.

For 6 to 8 carrot pieces per person

Either 36 to 48 baby carrots about 2 inches (5 cm) long, or 12 or more mature carrots

Cold water

2 Tb butter for cooking, plus 2 to 3 Tb for final flavoring

1 Tb very finely minced shallots or scallions

½ tsp salt, more as needed

Freshly ground white pepper

1 tsp sugar

Trim and peel the carrots. If you are using mature carrots, halve or quarter them and pare to nice baby carrot shapes (save trimmings for salads or soup). Arrange in a roomy saucepan with enough water to come halfway up the carrots. Add the initial 2 tablespoons butter, the shallots or scallions, salt, pepper, and sugar. Cover the pan and boil for 5 minutes (or longer for mature carrots) until liquid has evaporated and carrots are just tender—careful at the end that carrots don't scorch. Correct seasoning.

❶   May be cooked ahead. Set aside uncovered.

Shortly before serving, toss the carrots with the additional butter, so they are warmed through and glistening.

Tomatoes Moussakaise

Baked tomatoes stuffed with lamb and eggplant

I call these "moussakaise" because the stuffing is lamb and eggplant, and that's what makes a moussaka, a good accompaniment since there is not much meat on a rack of lamb. These stuffed tomatoes beef up the meal, so to speak.

For 6 tomato halves

1 firm shiny eggplant about 9 by 5 inches (23 by 13 cm)

Salt

A handful of parsley sprigs

1 or 2 cloves garlic, peeled

1 large onion, peeled and quartered

Olive oil or other cooking oil

The meat trimmings from the racks of lamb, or about 1½ cups (3½ dL; 12 ounces or 340 g) lean raw lamb stew meat

½ cup (1 dL) dry white wine or dry white French vermouth

1 cup (¼ L) chicken stock

½ tsp thyme (or rosemary, or mixed herbs, or tarragon)

3 large firm ripe tomatoes

Freshly ground pepper

Trimmings from racks of lamb make a delicious stuffing for accompanying tomatoes.

½ cup (1 dL) crumbs from crustless fresh
white nonsweet bread

Equipment:
**A food processor with steel blade makes quick
work of the chopping.**

Salting and draining the eggplant
Peel the eggplant and cut into dice ⅜ inch
(1 cm) to a side; toss in a large sieve with 1 teaspoon salt and let drain.

Chopping onion and lamb
Meanwhile, if you have a food processor, start
it running, and drop in the parsley, letting machine run for a few seconds until parsley is
chopped; scrape parsley into a small bowl and
reserve. (Do not bother to clean out processor
too thoroughly.) Start running it again, and
drop in the garlic; when minced, drop in the
onion, turning machine on and off in several
bursts until onion is chopped fairly fine. Film a
medium-sized frying pan (nonstick preferred)
with oil, turn the onion and garlic into it, and
sauté slowly. Divide the lamb into 2 batches
and grind 1 batch at a time with on-off spurts
in the processor, adding each as done to the
onion. (Otherwise, chop ingredients by hand,
using a meat grinder, if you wish, for the
lamb.)

Simmering the lamb
Sauté the lamb with the onion for a few minutes over moderately high heat, tossing and
turning, until lamb has browned lightly and
turned from red to gray; pour in the wine and
stock, and stir in the herbs. Cover and simmer
slowly for about half an hour, or until lamb is
tender and liquid has evaporated. Turn lamb
into a sieve set over a bowl, to drain out accumulated cooking fat.

The tomato shells
With a grapefruit knife, potato baller, or teaspoon, hollow out the tomatoes, leaving just
the outer flesh. Salt lightly, and reverse on a
rack to drain.

Finishing the stuffing
Dry the eggplant in paper towels; film the
frying pan again with oil, and sauté the
eggplant, tossing and turning, for several

minutes until tender. Return the lamb to the
pan with the eggplant and sauté a few minutes more, tossing and turning and letting the
mixture brown very lightly. Toss with the
minced parsley, and carefully correct seasoning.
🕐   Stuffing may be prepared a day in advance; refrigerate in a covered container.

Filling the tomatoes
Arrange the tomatoes hollow side up in an
oiled baking dish. Fill them with the stuffing,
spread on a spoonful of bread crumbs, and
drizzle a little oil over the tops.
🕐   May be prepared several hours in advance. Cover and refrigerate.

Baking—or broiling
10 minutes or less
The tomatoes need just a thorough heating
through, since the stuffing is all cooked and
you don't want the shells to burst. Set them
in the oven with the lamb, during its last bit
of cooking. (Or bake 10 minutes or so in a
400°F/205°C oven, or set under a low broiler.)
🕐   Tomatoes should be cooked only at the
last minute or they lose their shape.

*Tomatoes with lamb and eggplant stuffing make a nice
luncheon dish.*

Gratin of Potatoes à la Savoyarde—or à la Lyonnaise

Scalloped potatoes baked in broth with onions and cheese

Some kind of potato dish is very good with lamb, and I like this one cooked in broth, rather than in milk like the famous potatoes dauphinoise, since it is less rich—although the cheese does add a certain heft. However, the lamb morsels are so small!

For 6 people

Several Tb soft butter
2 to 3 cups (½ to ¾ L) thinly sliced onions
12 to 16 medium "boiling" potatoes, peeled and thinly sliced
Salt and freshly ground pepper
1½ cups (3½ dL) coarsely grated Swiss or mixed cheese
2 to 3 cups (½ to ¾ L) chicken stock

Equipment:
A food processor is useful for slicing onions and potatoes, or a hand slicer; a flameproof 2-quart (2-L) baking-and-serving dish, such as an oval one 9 by 12 by 2 inches (23 by 30 by 5 cm)

Assembling

Preheat oven to 425°F/220°C. Melt 2 tablespoons butter in a frying pan and sauté the onions slowly, stirring occasionally, while you peel and slice the potatoes. Smear the baking dish with butter and spread in a layer of potatoes, season lightly with salt and pepper, and spread in ⅓ of the onions (which need not be fully cooked), then ⅓ of the cheese. Continue with 2 more layers of potatoes, onions, and cheese, ending with the last of the cheese. Dot top with 2 tablespoons butter, and pour in enough chicken stock to come only halfway up the potatoes.

Baking
About 40 minutes

Set dish over moderately high heat on top of the stove, bring to the simmer, and place in lower middle level of preheated oven. Bake for 30 to 40 minutes. Ideally the liquid will have been almost entirely absorbed when the potatoes are tender; if not, remove baking dish from oven, tilt it, and draw out excess liquid with a bulb baster. Boil it down rapidly in a saucepan until thickened, pour it back into the dish, tilting in all directions, and return to oven for a few minutes to finish baking.

❶ If potatoes are to stay warm for half an hour or so, remove from oven when they are tender but there is still a little unabsorbed liquid in the dish; keep warm, loosely (never tightly) covered, over a pan of simmering water, on an electric hot tray, or in a warming oven.

Thinly sliced potatoes cook quickly.

Hazelnut Cornucopias

Rolled cookies—cookie horns—tuiles aux avelines

This is the type of cookie that is soft and pliable when it has just come from the oven, giving you several seconds to roll or form it into a shape before it crisps. The formula makes a nicely delicate wafer, and the flavor of toasted hazelnuts is particularly delicious. If you cannot find fine fresh hazelnuts, however, substitute walnuts—which can be ground without toasting. (*Note:* All shelled or ground nuts keep freshest in the freezer.)

*For about 16 cookies 4½ inches
(11½ cm) in diameter*

¾ cup (3 ounces or 85 g) shelled hazelnuts

½ cup (3½ ounces or 100 g) sugar

½ stick (2 ounces or 60 g) unsalted butter

⅛ tsp salt

2 Tb heavy cream

¼ cup (4 Tb or ½ dL) egg whites (about 2 whites)

4 level Tb (1¼ ounces or 35 g) all-purpose flour in a sifter

1 Tb dark Jamaica rum

A little soft butter

Equipment:

A blender or food processor (or nut chopper); 2 lightly buttered nonstick cookie sheets; a kitchen timer; a wide flexible spatula or a pancake turner; 3 or 4 metal cookie horns, or cornucopia shapes made from brown paper. Those illustrated here are 4½ inches long and 2 inches in diameter at the mouth (11½ by 5 cm); other sizes and shapes are illustrated at the end of the recipe.

Toasting and grinding the hazelnuts
(The hazelnuts are toasted to give additional flavor and also to loosen the outside skins; taste several to be sure they are not rancid.) Place them in a roasting pan and toast for 10 to 15 minutes in a preheated 350°F/180°C oven, stirring 2 or 3 times, until lightly browned. Rub by small handfuls in a towel to remove as much of their brown skins as you easily can. When cool, grind ⅓ of them roughly in a blender or food processor and set aside in a small bowl. Grind the rest of them with the sugar, and reserve for the following cookie mixture.

The cookie mixture
Preheat oven to 425°F/220°C, and set rack in middle level. Cream the butter in a mixing bowl (if chilled, cut into pieces and beat with a wooden spoon in a metal bowl over warm water; if it softens too much, then beat over cold water until a creamy mass). Blend in the sugar and hazelnut mixture, the salt, and the cream. Add the egg whites, stirring only enough to blend. Sift and fold in the flour by thirds, then fold in the rum. Mixture should look like a heavy batter.

🕐   Batter should be used promptly.

Forming, baking, and rolling the cookies
Before forming the cookies, be sure the oven is preheated, have your spatula and your metal or paper molds ready, and have your kitchen timer handy. Drop a 2-tablespoon blob of cookie mixture on a buttered cookie sheet, and spread it out, as illustrated, into a 4½-inch

There's room for only three cookies on this standard-sized nonstick baking sheet.

(11½-cm) circle with the back of a tablespoon, making sure that the edges are the same thickness as the rest of the shape, or about ¹/₁₆ inch (¼ cm). Form 1 or 2 more cookie shapes, leaving a good inch (2½ cm) between them. Sprinkle a pinch of chopped hazelnuts over each. Place in oven and set timer for 4 minutes, meanwhile forming another sheet of cookies.

Cookies are done when about ¼ inch (¾ cm) around edges is lightly browned (if they seem to be cooking too fast, lower oven thermostat slightly). Set cookie sheet on open oven door and let cool a few seconds. One at a time gently slither spatula or pancake turner under a cookie all around to loosen it, lift it off, turn it upside down on your work surface, and roll it around the metal or paper horn. Rapidly repeat with the other cookies—leaving them on the oven door keeps them pliable until you are ready to roll them.

Close oven door and wait for oven to come up to temperature again, then bake the other sheet, and form another batch. Meanwhile, in less than a minute, the rolled cookies will have crisped and you can gently dislodge the molds. Let cookies cool on a rack.

🕐 These cookies are fragile, and soften rapidly in damp weather. Bake them shortly before serving, or store in a warming oven at around 100°F/38°C, or freeze them.

Variations:
You can roll the cookies into other shapes, such as cylinders, using the end of a wooden spoon or a cylindrical cookie form. You can press the limp cookie over the outside of a small bowl or inside a teacup to make cookie cups. You can make the classic tile or *tuile* shape, when you drape the limp cookie over a rolling pin to crisp. Or, of course, you can serve them perfectly plain and flat—which makes them easier to store, and nice with tea or sherbets.

Work quickly while cookies are still warm and pliable. Use a metal form for rolling cookies or make one out of brown paper.

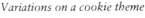

Variations on a cookie theme

Fresh Strawberries and Cream-filled Hazelnut Cornucopias

For 6 people

About 2 quarts (2 L) beautiful fresh ripe strawberries

2 egg whites, a pinch of salt, and a pinch of cream of tartar

½ pint (¼ L) heavy cream, chilled

About 2 cups (½ L) confectioners sugar, sifted

Pure vanilla extract, or dark Jamaica rum, or kirsch

6 hazelnut cornucopias (preceding recipe), plus more, if you wish, to pass with the berries

2 Tb chopped toasted hazelnuts (preceding recipe)

Equipment:

A clean dry bowl for whipping egg whites, and a large wire whip or portable beater; a second bowl, of metal, for whipping cream, set into a larger bowl with a tray of ice cubes and water to cover them

The reason for rolling the preceding hazelnut wafers into cornucopias is so that you can fill them with a light whipped cream and serve them with strawberries. You dip the berries by their stems into powdered sugar, and then into the cream—lovely finger food for all ages. However, plain whipped cream all by itself is, I think, so rich that I like it lightened with some beaten egg whites, which also serves to stabilize the cream.

The strawberries

If strawberries are sandy, drop them into a bowl of cold water, swish them gently, then lift out immediately and drain on a rack. Pick them over to be sure each is perfect, but do not stem them.

Whipped cream lightened with egg whites

Shortly before serving, beat the egg whites until they start foaming, then beat in the salt and cream of tartar, and continue beating until egg whites form stiff peaks. Set egg whites aside and immediately start whipping the cream, using the same beater—circulate it all around the bowl, incorporating as much air as possible, and whip until cream holds its shape nicely but is not too stiff. Fold in enough of the egg whites by dollops to lighten the cream, but it should hold its shape sufficiently to be spooned into the cornucopias. Fold in confectioners sugar to taste—2 to 3 tablespoons, and 1 teaspoon or so of vanilla, rum, or kirsch. (Complete information on egg whites, page 109; on cream, page 108.)

🕐 Strawberries may be prepared and left on their rack an hour or so in advance—refrigerate them on a hot day. If the cream is made somewhat ahead, turn it into a sieve lined with washed cheesecloth and set over a bowl; cover with plastic wrap and refrigerate—it will exude a little milky liquid.

Serving

The moment before serving, arrange the berries in a bowl or on plates. Fill the cornucopias with the cream, using a teaspoon or a pastry bag, and sprinkle a pinch of chopped nuts over the top of the cream; arrange the cornucopias in a bowl, as illustrated. Serve at once, passing separately bowls of powdered sugar and the remaining cream plus, if you wish, additional cornucopias or, better, the same cookie but in one of the other shapes illustrated on page 67.

🕐 *Timing*

You will need a few—a very few—extra minutes between each course of this dinner. Before dessert, you'd fill and arrange the cookies; take your time, they're fragile. Before the main course, first you'd take the lamb out of the oven. It will sit and re-absorb its juices while you change plates, toss the carrots in hot butter, garnish your warm platter, and bring forth the gratin. Surely you'll want to parade the stylish lamb platter around the table and then carve it right there, which takes seconds. Courses like these shouldn't follow like railroad cars anyway, jolt, jolt, jolt; they should be set apart by a tender moment of memory and anticipation.

If you have only one oven, do the potatoes ahead, and keep them warm while roasting the lamb. Or cook them partially and let them finish with the lamb. Ideally, the lamb should undergo its second stage of roasting, accompanied with the tomatoes, while you're enjoying the first course.

Just before dinner, then, set the crumbed and basted lamb back in the oven with the tomatoes. Just before that, sauce the shellfish and spoon into the artichoke halves, and arrange the strawberries in their bowl (strawberries can bruise each other so they're better fixed not too far ahead).

An hour before dinner (on the one-oven plan), the lamb gets seared; then the oven temperature is lowered and the potatoes are sliced and the gratin mixed and baked, while the lamb sits at room temperature. At this time you'd whip the cream and refrigerate it in a cheesecloth-lined sieve over a bowl, and make the sauce for your shellfish.

That morning, you would prepare the lamb for the oven and refrigerate it, cook the onions for the gratin, cook the carrots, and hollow, stuff, and refrigerate the tomatoes.

The day before, you trim the lamb, make sauce with the bones, and prepare the tomato stuffing. That day, or even the day before that, you can cook and refrigerate the artichokes.

The cookies can be made any time and frozen; just bear in mind that the batter should be baked right after mixing.

Menu Variations

See Mournful Remarks preceding the *artichoke scoops* recipe for artichoke-filling possibilities (and problems). Mayonnaise alone might be too rich, but you could simply spoon a little vinaigrette into the artichoke cavities. Or mound the scoops with highly seasoned egg or fish salad. An alternative would be asparagus, either hot or cold, or tucked into puff pastry rectangles as we did on the first series of the *Company* shows.

I can't think of any main dish so elegant as *rack of lamb*—and that's the point of this whole dinner.

As for *vegetables,* we chose the potato gratin for ideal flavor, and the others chiefly for their looks. You could stuff onions with the de-lectable lamb and eggplant mixture, and serve cherry tomatoes cooked in butter with herbs. If they're small enough to be served one apiece, stuff your eggplant cases. The old-fashioned thing was to carve the racks and make a pal-isade, like a crown roast, around a heap of mashed potatoes, then put a paper frill on each rib end. Too thumby-looking for me.

The *cookie* recipe works perfectly with walnuts, if you can't get really fresh hazelnuts; and the cookies can be formed into several shapes, as suggested at the end of the recipe. If you made cookie cups, you might fill them with raspberries or blueberries, and pass whipped cream separately. Or you could make the *vacherins* on page 32, but very small ones, fill them with the cream, and surround each with strawberries.

Leftovers

Cooked *artichokes* keep for 2 or 3 days. If you have spare ones, try slicing the bases and serv-ing them in a thickened vinaigrette with scal-lops "cooked" in lime juice. Or mix artichoke bits into a salad. Extra shellfish can be minced and mixed with mayonnaise for a cocktail dip or spread.

Extra cooked *lamb ribs* are the cook's precious property. Bare your teeth and snarl, until lunch tomorrow.

Cooked *carrots* can be reheated, briefly. Or wash them off and dice them for a cold vegetable *macédoine*, or for a soup garnish. The *potato gratin* can be reheated, and so can the *tomatoes*—chop them and serve on toast.

As for the *dessert,* cookies freeze, and you can purée the strawberries, mix with extra cream, and freeze for a strawberry mousse.

Postscript: Two budget cuts of lamb

Flanks and Breast of Lamb:
Although a rack of lamb is costly indeed, the lamb flank, which is the continuation of the rack down the belly of the beast, sometimes comes free with the rack. If not, it costs ⅕ as much, which is very reasonable. The breast of lamb corresponds to the brisket of beef; it is the flank and its continuation toward the front.

Separate fatty flank ribs from whole brisket, then loosen breastbone from ribs before cooking; remove it afterward.

Broiled or Barbecued Lamb Flanks

Epigrammes d'agneau

For 4 to 6 people — 2 lamb flanks
Peel and cut fell (outside membrane) and fat from top of flanks; slit open and remove excess fat from inside. Cut the flanks into serving pieces, leaving riblets in the meat. Brown lightly in a frying pan in a little oil, with a chopped carrot and onion. Pour out browning fat, add half-and-half white wine or vermouth and chicken stock barely to cover the meat. Add a clove of garlic, an imported bay leaf, and a little dried thyme. Cover and simmer slowly for about an hour, or until lamb is tender. Remove to a platter, arrange in 1 layer, and set a pan and weight on top, to flatten the meat, which will have curled out of shape during its cooking. Leave for 20 to 30 minutes.

When ready to broil, cover 1 side of each piece with the mustard coating described for the racks of lamb, page 61, and spread on a layer of fresh bread crumbs and a drizzle of melted butter. When ready to cook, set for several minutes under a hot broiler until heated through and nicely browned.

You could boil down the braising liquid, after degreasing it, and serve it as a sauce; or keep it in the freezer for the next time you need a sauce for lamb.

Lamb flanks may also be barbecued.

Stuffed Braised Breast of Lamb

For 4 to 6 people
The breast of lamb contains the boat-shaped breastbone with a number of auxiliary bones attached, and some riblets. Leave the riblets in, but detach the breastbone from them; remove breastbone after cooking. Slice off the fell and fat from outside the meat. Cut a pocket the length of the meat going under the rib bones, removing any fat layers you can reach inside.

Use a rice and lamb or sausage stuffing, or bread crumb stuffing, or the lamb and eggplant stuffing suggested for the tomatoes on page 63. Sew or skewer the stuffing into the pocket left by the breastbone. Brown and braise the breast for about an hour, as described for the flanks in the preceding recipe — you may wish to add a peeled and chopped tomato or 2 along with the rest of the ingredients. Serve with a dish of fresh beets or a salad, for a hearty informal meal.

Breast of lamb, stuffed and braised, makes its own savory sauce.

Classic, delicate, and perfect for a fine day in June . . . or November, for that matter

Summer Dinner

Menu
For 6 people

A Platter of Chicken Livers Molded in Aspic

✤

*Individual Fresh Salmon Steaks, Poached,
and Served with Hollandaise Sauce*
New Potatoes
*Cucumber Triangles Sautéed in Butter
and Dill*

✤

*Savarin au Rhum et aux Fruits Exotiques —
The giant ring-shaped cousin of rum
baba, filled with a selection of tropical
fruits*

✤

Suggested wines:
*A light dry white with the first course, like a
riesling or muscadet. A fine full white with
the salmon, like a Meursault, Corton
Charlemagne, or well-aged chardonnay. A
sparkling wine with the dessert—semisweet
Champagne, Vouvray mousseux, Asti
spumante*

If we were serving this meal in cool weather, when it would certainly taste just as good, we might begin with hot consommé. But in warm weather, what could seem more piquant and inviting than these small oval aspics, clear as fine amber, set around a jackstraw pile of finely slivered crisp string beans? These fanciful trifles have a festive air, though their decoration is a simple matter, and the poached chicken livers, mysteriously brooding within, are delicately flavorful. Delicacy is, indeed, crucial, because salmon has so much character that it must dominate any menu on which it appears.

Since salmon has become increasingly expensive, we rarely buy a whole fish anymore; rather, we offer salmon steaks. In America, green peas from the garden are the classic accompaniment, especially on the Fourth of July, when salmon is traditionally eaten. Some prefer it with fresh asparagus; some like it cold, with mayonnaise and a cucumber salad. I like the cucumber idea, and agree with Scandinavian cooks that dill is the herb of choice with salmon. So we'll have our cukes cooked very lightly in dill and butter, dished up fragrant and crisp, with a golden hollandaise for pink fish and green vegetable. Cold salmon is delightful, but here, we want it at its most glorious—in other words, hot. The platter looks particularly appetizing—appearance matters so much in summer meals! And you can't have boiled salmon without boiled potatoes, especially new ones cooked in their tender skins.

Our fish is a Pacific salmon, *Oncorhynchus*, 3 of whose species, the silver, sockeye, and pink, are most commonly found in fishmarkets. To acquire its Atlantic cousin, *Salmo salar*, you generally have to pack up your waders and head for Nova Scotia or Iceland. Wild salmon are rare these days, because for a century we failed to take into account their very special habits, and to preserve the complex environment they require. They're anadromous, meaning that they live and grow in the ocean but spawn in fresh water: always in the very water where they themselves were spawned. This may mean a tremendous journey upstream, leaping up falls or fish ladders built into dams. If the stream is obstructed or polluted, the salmon can't make it. Just lately, though, salmon have been found in rivers that

The best way to get at the mango (left) is to slice it in strips off its clinging flat oval seed. The kiwi (bottom) looks like a small potato; what a surprise to cut into it and find juicy-green flower-patterned flesh. The mild-mannered papaya (top right) is packed with peppery black seeds.

had not known them for a century: children of spawn planted there by the U.S. Fish and Wildlife Service. Hope springs eternal!

Strawberries follow salmon on so many menus; though they'd be delicious with a savarin cake, we've opted this time for the doubly summery taste of tropical fruits, adding enormous black grapes to set off the green of kiwi fruit and the orange of mango and papaya. A few black grapes are saved, to be lightly frosted with sugar and set becomingly around the glazed, gleaming, rum-soaked cake. The traditional decoration is crystallized fruits, but I haven't found good ones here lately, and I wasn't foresighted enough to order replenishments from France. If you want the real thing, fruits big and brilliant as crown jewels and tasting intensely *like* fruit—not like rubber baby-buggy bumpers—you can write to Maiffret, Fabrique de Fruits Confits et Chocolats, 5 3, rue d'Antibes, 06400, Cannes, France, a house of master craftsmen that does a worldwide mail-order business.

As for the cake itself, it's made of the same simple batter as the more familiar small *babas au rhum,* a confection that is supposed to have been invented in the seventeenth century by the amiable king of Poland, Stanislas Leszczyński, the French queen's father. Some say he named it for Ali Baba; but "baba" in Polish means "little granny," and I like the cozy thought. In the nineteenth century, a Parisian pastry cook baked the batter in a large ring mold and named it "savarin" in honor of the gastronome Brillat-Savarin. This too is a cozy thought: Savarin was a delightful man who named his favorite horse Joyous, who traveled in the American colonies and loved both us and our food. While here, in the woods near Hartford, he even shot a wild turkey, which he cooked and served to his American hosts. His book, *The Physiology of Taste,* translated by M. F. K. Fisher (New York: Alfred A. Knopf, 1971), is well worth any food lover's time some fragrant summer evening, made serene by a dinner like this one.

Preparations and Marketing

Recommended Equipment:

To jell small, manageable amounts of aspic, use a small saucepan you can quickly chill in a bowl of ice and water. To form the aspics, we used 6 oval molds, metal for easier unmolding, of ½-cup (1-dL-plus) capacity; you could use round molds, or large muffin tins. You'll need a tray to put the molds on.

To cook the salmon, use a pan big enough to hold all 6 steaks in 4 inches (10 cm) water, plus a kitchen timer, a skimmer, and a clean kitchen towel.

To make hollandaise, have 2 small stainless-steel saucepans and a wire whip.

For the cucumbers, a large frying pan, not of cast iron, and for the potatoes, a deep saucepan with lid.

The savarin recipe is for a 4-cup (1-L) mold. You don't need a special one; even a bumpy ring mold will do, or a cake pan or soufflé dish. The dough can be made by hand, but an electric mixer with a dough hook is helpful (dough is too soft and sticky for a food processor). To drench the cake with syrup, have a bulb baster; to glaze it, a pastry brush.

Staples to Have on Hand:

Salt
White peppercorns
Sugar
Dried tarragon
Optional: pure vanilla extract
Wine vinegar
Strong consommé or beef bouillon (1 cup or
    ¼ L, or more)
Butter (3 sticks; 12 ounces or 340 g)

Eggs (5 "large")
Dry-active yeast (1 package or 1 Tb)
All-purpose flour (1 ⅓ to 1 ½ cups or 190 to
    215 g)
Carrot (1 large)
Fresh dill or parsley
Lemons (1)
Port or Madeira wine (½ cup or 1 dL)
Dark Jamaica rum, kirsch, or bourbon whiskey

Specific Ingredients for This Menu:

Perfect whole chicken livers (6)
Salmon steaks (6, weighing 8 ounces or 225 g
    each, and ¾ inch or 2 cm thick) ▼
Wine-flavored aspic (recipe on page 109; 4 to
    6 cups or 1 to 1 ½ L)
Fresh green peas (1 cup or ¼ L podded)
Cucumbers (3 large)
New potatoes (18 to 24, 1 ½ inches or 4 cm in
    diameter)
Apricot jam (1 ½ cups or 3 ½ dL)
Fruits to fill savarin ▼
Optional: green beans (½ pound or 225 g)

Poached salmon with hollandaise sauce and dilled cucumbers

▶   **Remarks:**

Salmon: except for the color of skin and flesh, what follows applies to the buying and storing of any fresh fish. The scales should be shiny and fresh, and the skin color bright—bright silver for the lovely salmon. The eyes are bright and bulging—never buy fish when the eyes are flat or sunken—and the gills red . . . that is, if the head is on. The meat is red-orange—a deeper color if you can get the sublime King or Chinook Pacific salmon—and has a glossy sheen, and it feels firm and fresh to the touch, with a little give when pressed. A fish that is past its prime of freshness will begin to soften, its skin will lose its bright silvery color, the scales will be dry and dull, and the flesh will pale—an enzyme action is taking its toll on texture and flavor. Smell it; perfectly fresh fish has either no odor, or else a very mild, delicious one.

A good fishmarket doesn't stop at refrigerating its wares; the fish are bedded on ice. Do likewise. Rush it home (or have a plastic ice container with you), and place it in a plastic bag surrounded with ice, in a bowl, and refrigerate it. Drain out accumulated ice water, renew ice 2 or 3 times a day, and really fresh fish will keep well for 2 or 3 days; but, of course, the sooner you cook it the better.

Fruits to fill savarin: if you decide to use the tropical fruits shown here, be sure to buy them several days in advance. Kiwi fruit, mangoes, and papayas are all sold unripe; put them in a closed paper bag or a ripening container at room temperature, with a ripe apple or tomato for company if you want to hasten the process. You can judge the ripeness of mangoes, papayas, or kiwis by giving a gentle squeeze. They should feel like a ripe peach.

Chicken Livers in Aspic

Jellied anything, from consommé to eggs in aspic, is an inviting summer prospect, and these attractive chicken liver molds could serve as the main dish for a luncheon in any season, as well as being the first course for our summer dinner.

Timing: if you have never done this kind of thing before, it may look too difficult for any but a professional to tackle. However, it is purely an assembly job, the sole requirements being plenty of time, ice, room in the refrigerator, and quite a bit more aspic than you think you will need. You can take as little as an hour or as much as a day or 2 to complete the very simple steps here—5 in all—which consist of making layers of aspic and objects layered in aspic: each layer has to chill in the refrigerator until it sets—a matter of 10 to 15 minutes. Then the molds need an hour or more of overall setting time to be sure they are thoroughly jelled and can safely be unmolded. Aspic, by the way, is a liquid—consommé in this case—that has gone through a clarification process to render it clear and sparkling, and gelatin has been added to it so that it sets or jells as it chills.

Clear wine-flavored aspic holds poached chicken liver in gleaming display.

Ingredients Note: The better your aspic, the more delicious your final result. You can make it all yourself, or use canned chicken broth or canned consommé plus Port or Madeira wine, or a simmering of either with white wine and aromatic vegetables. What you use depends on your resources.

For 6 people

6 perfect whole chicken livers

1 cup (¼ L) strong fine consommé or beef bouillon

½ cup (1 dL) Port or Madeira wine (or consommé)

½ tsp dried tarragon

4 to 6 cups (1 to 1½ L) wine-flavored aspic (page 109)

Decorative suggestions (see others in Menu Variations): 1 large cooked carrot and 1 cup (¼ L) cooked green peas

Garnishing suggestions: ½ pound (225 g) green beans, blanched and finely julienned (optional)

Equipment:

6 oval or round molds or cups of about ½-cup (1-dL-plus) capacity, preferably of metal for easy unmolding—or you could use muffin tins; a small metal saucepan set in a bowl of ice and water

Poaching the chicken livers
To be done in advance
Pick over the chicken livers, removing any discolored spots and bits of fat. Place in a small saucepan with the consommé or bouillon, the wine, and the tarragon. Bring to the simmer, and cook at just below the simmer (water is shivering but not really bubbling) for 8 minutes. Cover loosely and let cool in the liquid—to pick up added flavor—for at least half an hour, or overnight. Drain, and chill.

The aspic

Prepare the aspic, and be sure to test it out—pour a little into a saucer, chill for 20 minutes, then fork it out onto a plate and leave 10 minutes or so at room temperature to be sure it will hold its own. On a warm day you may find you'll need a little more gelatin: 1 tablespoon for 1 ½ cups (3 ½ dL) liquid.

The decorations

I have chosen some very simple decorations here: the carrot slices go into the bottom of the mold over its aspic lining, and the peas go in at the end, so that when the aspic is unmolded all is reversed. Cut several gashes down the length of the carrot, so that when you then cut the carrot into thin rounds you'll get a decorative edging: if you wish, also make half moons out of other rounds. Place on a saucer. Slip the skins off the peas, and pick them in half—they separate easily; place in a small bowl. Chill both carrots and peas.

Assembling

Have your main supply of aspic liquefied in a pan or bowl; the reason for the small saucepan over ice is so that you can chill just what you need, until it is almost syrupy and about to set. When you have used that up, you pour a little more into the pan, chill, and continue. Otherwise you would be warming and then chilling such a large amount that your assembling would take hours to do.

Making chicken livers in aspic—the sequence of events from lower left to right and the ingredients above them

Set your molds on a tray, and pour a ¼-inch (¾-cm) layer of aspic into them. Make room in the refrigerator, and set tray on a perfectly level place; chill until set—10 to 15 minutes.

Pour a little aspic into the small saucepan, chill over ice until cold to your finger but not jelled. Spear a carrot round with the point of a small knife, dip into the cold aspic, and center into a mold, adding other carrot pieces if you wish. When all decorations are in place, set in the refrigerator for a few minutes until anchored.

Arrange the chilled livers in the molds, pour in ½ inch or so (1 ½ cm) cold aspic, and chill. (If you poured in tepid aspic, that could melt the bottom layer and the decorations would float up.)

When set, spoon in more cold aspic to cover the livers.

When that has set, in 10 to 15 minutes, spoon on a layer of peas, and fill the molds with cold aspic.

Chill for at least an hour, until thoroughly set.

🕐   May be assembled 2 or 3 days in advance of serving; cover with plastic wrap and keep chilled.

Serving

If you have allowed for enough aspic, you can use the remainder to decorate your plates or platter. Pour it into a pan to make a layer about ⅜ inch (1 cm) thick, and chill. Just before arranging the serving, cut the chilled aspic, still in its pan, into dice or diamonds or other shapes, or simply turn the whole sheet of aspic out onto your work surface and chop it with a knife. In the arrangement on page 72, the molds have been dipped, one by one, into hot water for 8 to 10 seconds, or just long enough to loosen the aspic, and they have then been unmolded onto the serving platter, with chopped aspic all around and a central spray of cooked shredded green beans.

Fresh Salmon Steaks, Poached

Plain poaching, or boiling as it is sometimes erroneously called, is certainly one of the easiest and most delicious ways to cook perfectly fresh fine salmon. Nothing disturbs its lovely natural flavors, and there are no pitfalls I can think of in its cooking.

For 6 people

6 salmon steaks 8 ounces (225 g) each and about ¾ inch (2 cm) thick (I prefer boneless steaks cut from the fillet, skin on)

2 tsp salt and 2 Tb wine vinegar per quart or liter cooking water

Sprigs of fresh dill or parsley

Ready accompaniments: the hollandaise sauce, boiled new potatoes, and sautéed cucumbers (following recipes)

Equipment:

Pliers or tweezers; a wide saucepan, chicken fryer, or roaster with about 4 inches (10 cm) boiling water; a kitchen timer; a large skimmer for removing the fish; a clean kitchen towel; a soup spoon and fork; a heated platter and something to cover it with

Preparing the salmon

Run your finger searchingly over tops and sides of fish, and if you feel any big or little bones, pull them out with pliers or tweezers.

Otherwise there is nothing to do, since the fish will be skinned after poaching. Keep on ice until the moment of cooking.

Poaching the fish
8 to 10 minutes

About 15 minutes before you plan to serve, have the water at the boil, and pour in the salt and vinegar. Bring back to the boil, and lay in the salmon, piece by piece and skin side down. Set timer for 8 minutes. Regulate heat so water never comes near the boil again but stays at the shiver—no real bubbles, but a slight movement in the water to show it's cooking. When time is up, turn off the heat and let salmon rest for 2 minutes (or a few minutes longer if you are not ready to serve).

Peeling the salmon and placing it on the platter

With a folded towel in one hand, lift a piece of salmon out of the water with your skimmer; turn fish flesh side down on the towel. Place on your work surface, and lift off the skin with spoon and fork. Using the towel, reverse the steak right side up on the skimmer, and set on the hot serving dish. Cover and proceed rapidly with the rest of the salmon steaks. If your platter is large enough, you may wish to spoon a garland of cooked cucumbers around the fish, lay a ribbon of hollandaise down the center, and decorate that with wisps of fresh dill or parsley. Then pass the rest of the sauce, and the potatoes, separately.

🕐 The cooked fish can safely wait in its cooking water for 15 minutes or so, but once peeled and plattered serve it immediately.

Salmon steaks take only eight minutes to cook.

Skin peels off easily after poaching.

Hollandaise Sauce

Although blenders and food processors do a quick and easy hollandaise, a good cook should be absolutely confident about whipping up a hollandaise by hand. It not only takes less than 5 minutes, but you are saved the time-consuming and messy task of scraping as much sauce as you can off prickly machine blades while getting it all over your fingers. With a handmade sauce all you need do is bang the whip on the side of the pan, scrape the sauce up in 2 or 3 scoops with a rubber spatula, and it's out in a neat matter of seconds. Counting everything from start to clean-up, I conclude it's faster by hand.

For about 1½ cups (3½ dL), serving 6

1½ to 2 sticks (6 to 8 ounces or 180 to 225 g) butter
3 egg yolks
The grated rind of 1 lemon (optional)
1 Tb fresh lemon juice; more if needed
1 Tb water or fish-poaching liquid
¼ tsp salt, or more as needed
Big pinch white pepper; more as needed
2 Tb additional butter
1 Tb or so fish-poaching liquid and/or cream (optional)

Preliminaries
Have all your ingredients and equipment at hand. Melt the 1½ to 2 sticks butter in a small saucepan, and you are ready to begin.

Thickening the egg yolks before heating
To prepare the egg yolks for their ordeal, place them in a stainless-steel pan and beat vigorously with a wire whip for a good minute, until they have thickened into a cream.

Adding the flavorings
Beat in the optional lemon rind, the lemon juice, and the water or fish-poaching liquid, along with the ¼ teaspoon salt and pinch of pepper. Add the 2 tablespoons additional butter as is; by melting slowly as you proceed in the next step, the butter will discourage the eggs from suffering heat shock, which might curdle them.

Thickening the yolks over heat
1 to 2 minutes
(Your object here will be to warm the yolks slowly enough so that they will thicken into a smooth creamy custard—too sudden or too prolonged heat will scramble them, and they cannot then absorb the melted butter to come. Remember you have complete control of your pan: you can lift it up from the heat, or set it aside, or even set the bottom of the pan in cold water to stop the cooking process at any time.)

Set pan over moderate heat and stir with your wire whip, reaching all over bottom of pan and taking about ½ second to complete each circuit. As the yolks slowly heat they will begin to foam—keep testing them with your finger, and when they feel hot, they are almost ready. Watch for a wisp of steam rising from the surface, which will also indicate their almost readiness. As soon as egg yolks have warmed, thickened, and creamed—which will happen suddenly—remove from heat and beat for a minute to cool them and stop the cooking.

Adding the butter
1 to 2 minutes
By droplets, beat the melted butter into the warm egg yolks, just as though you were making a mayonnaise—it is important to go slowly here, particularly at first, or the yolks cannot absorb the butter. Use as much butter as you wish, up to the maximum, to make a thick creamy sauce. Taste carefully for seasoning, adding more lemon juice, salt, and pepper as needed. To lighten the sauce, if you wish to, beat in droplets of warm fish-cooking liquid and/or cream.

Ahead-of-Time Notes: If you are doing the sauce in advance, beat in only 1 stick butter; then, just before serving, heat the remainder and beat it into the sauce. Less butter makes the sauce safer to hold, and the hot butter at the end will warm it nicely. To hold the sauce, leave at room temperature if the wait is but a few minutes, since hollandaise is served barely warm, never hot. Otherwise set it near a gas pilot light, or near a simmering pot, or in a pan of tepid (not hot) water. Remember that too much heat will gradually coagulate the egg yolks, they will release the butter from suspension, and the sauce will curdle. Remember also that it is dangerous to let a hollandaise sit around in the kitchen for more than an hour or so because egg yolks are fine breeding grounds for nasty bacteria.

Trouble Shooting:

If sauce refuses to thicken or if finished sauce thins out or curdles, sometimes the beating in of a tablespoon of cold water or an ice cube will bring it back. If not, beat a teaspoon of lemon juice and a tablespoon of the sauce in a small bowl until they cream and thicken, then drop by drop at first, beat in the rest of the sauce until you again have a creamy mass. However, if you have overheated the sauce and curdled the yolks, the best thing to do is to heat it more until they release most of their butter; strain it out, then start over using fresh egg yolks but the same butter.

Hollandaise sauce: beat in butter by dribbles at first, to make a thick cream.

Boiled New Potatoes

I like boiling rather than steaming for new potatoes because it seems to me that steaming can discolor them. In any case, they are easy indeed to cook and any leftovers can make a happy reappearance in a salad.

For 6 people

18 to 24 small new potatoes about 1½ inches (4 cm) in diameter

Salt

2 to 3 Tb butter

Equipment:

A saucepan large enough to hold potatoes comfortably, and with a lid; a larger saucepan to hold the first if potatoes must wait a bit

Wash the potatoes and pick them over, removing any blemishes with a knife. Arrange in saucepan and cover with cold water, adding 1½ teaspoons salt per quart or liter of water. About 35 minutes before you plan to serve them, cover and bring to a boil and maintain at a slow boil for about 25 minutes, or until potatoes are just tender when pierced with a sharp knife—eat one as a test if you are not sure. Drain out water, roll about gently over heat to dry them off, then roll with a little butter to glaze them.

These potatoes are at their best when served soon after cooking. If they must wait a bit, bring a little water to the simmer in the other pan, and set the potato pan in it, covering it loosely—potatoes must have air circulation or they will develop an off taste.

Cucumber Triangles Sautéed in Butter and Dill

The light fresh crunch of cucumbers and the flavor of dill seem always wedded to salmon. Here the cucumbers are cut, then tossed in butter and seasonings, with a sprinkling of dill. They still retain a bit of a crunch, and gain yet a different degree of cucumber flavor from being cooked.

For 6 people

3 large fine cucumbers

2 Tb or more butter

Salt and white pepper

2 to 3 Tb minced fresh dill, or a little dried dill weed and minced fresh parsley

Equipment:

A large frying pan, not of cast iron

Peel the cucumbers, slice in half lengthwise, and scoop out the seeds. Cut each half in half lengthwise, and then into triangles, as shown.

🕐   May be prepared several hours in advance; refrigerate in a covered bowl.

Not more than 10 minutes before serving, melt the butter in the pan, add the cucumbers, and toss over moderately high heat, seasoning lightly with salt, until cucumbers are almost cooked through but still retain some crunch. Season to taste with more salt, pepper, and, if you wish, toss with a tablespoon or 2 more butter. Then toss with sprinklings of dill.

🕐   Cucumbers should be served promptly or they lose both their crunch and their freshly cooked look.

Peeled and seeded cucumbers are cut into triangles, which make attractive shapes around the salmon platter.

Savarin aux Fruits Exotiques

A large ring-shaped yeast cake drenched in rum syrup and filled with a mixture of tropical fruits

Timing and Manufacturing Notes: The savarin is made of a simple yeast dough that when cooked makes a plain, dry cake that is strangely tasteless and coarse—purposely so, since its role is to be a sponge that will absorb an enormous amount of flavored syrup without collapsing. Given time to drink its fill, the savarin's every bite is deliciously moist, quite unlike anything else but the rum babas following this recipe.

Timing: you will need a minimum of 4½ hours: 1½ to 2 hours for the dough to rise in a bowl, 1 hour for it to rise in its mold, ½ hour for it to bake and cool, and a final hour for it to absorb its syrup and to drain before you can glaze and serve it. However, you can bake it ahead and freeze it; you can syrup and drain it in advance; you can glaze it ahead, as well.

Savarin dough can be baked and served in many ways: classic savarin with whipped cream and glacéed fruit (lower left), individual savarins and a rum baba (the cylindrical one), and our savarin with exotic fruits (top).

Avoiding dough troubles: be sure to dissolve your yeast in tepid water—hot water can kill it—and see that it is fully liquefied or it cannot do its work. Do not kill the yeast, either, by pouring hot butter on it. Give the dough time to rise; it may take longer than the amounts specified—it's the volume of the rise that you're looking for, not the time it takes to rise. Measure your flour correctly.

For 6 to 8 people

Dough for a 4-cup (1-L) Mold:
1 package (1 Tb) dry-active yeast
3 Tb tepid water (not over 110°F/43°C)
2 "large" eggs
2 Tb sugar
⅛ tsp salt
4 Tb tepid melted butter
1⅓ to 1½ cups (190 to 215 g) all-purpose flour—scoop dry-measure cups into flour and sweep off excess

The Rum Syrup:
2 cups (½ L) water
1 cup (¼ L; 7 ounces or 190 to 200 g) sugar
½ cup (1 dL) dark Jamaica rum, kirsch, or bourbon whiskey, or 2 to 3 Tb pure vanilla extract

Glazing and Filling:

1 ½ cups (3 ½ dL) apricot jam
4 Tb sugar
Mixed fruits such as 1 or 2 ripe mangoes, papayas, and kiwis, plus a small bunch of black grapes
Additional sugar as needed
Rum, kirsch, bourbon, or lemon juice to flavor the fruits (optional)
1 or 2 egg whites

Equipment:

A 2-quart (2-L) mixing bowl, or an electric mixer with dough hook; a 4-cup (1-L) savarin mold (illustrated), or other ring mold (or a cake pan or soufflé dish); a skewer; a bulb baster; a pastry brush

The Dough:
About 3 hours
Preliminaries
Stir the yeast into the tepid water and let dissolve completely while preparing the rest of the ingredients as follows. If eggs are chilled, warm them for 2 minutes in hot water, then break into mixing bowl. Blend in the sugar, salt, and butter. Measure the flour into the bowl, and stir in the completely liquefied yeast mixture.

Method for kneading by hand
Blend ingredients together with a rubber spatula or wooden spoon, and when too heavy to stir, begin kneading by hand: lift the dough with one hand, your fingers held together and curved like a spoon. Slap the dough against the side of the bowl, and vig-orously repeat the process for a dozen sticky passes or more, until the dough begins to take on some body, and finally enough for it to be removed from the bowl. (This is sup-posed to be a soft and sticky dough, but if it is still too soft after vigorous kneading, work in a little more flour; if too stiff, knead in droplets of milk.) Remove dough to your work surface, and let rest 2 to 3 minutes while you wash and dry the bowl. Knead the dough again by slapping it against your work surface, pushing it out with the heel of your hand, and continuing vigorously for a minute or 2 until it begins to peel itself cleanly from your fingers—it should stick to them if you hold a pinch of it, however. It will have enough elasticity so that you can grab it in both hands, pull it out, and give it a full twist without its breaking.

Method for kneading by electric mixer
Knead at moderate speed for several minutes until dough has enough body to ball on the dough hook or beater. (If too soft or too stiff see preceding paragraph.) Remove from mixer, wash out bowl, and finish by hand, as described.

The initial rise
About 2 hours
Roll the dough into a ball and return it to the mixing bowl. Cover with plastic wrap and let rise at around 75°F/24°C until the dough has doubled in bulk and feels light, spongy—1 ½ to 2 hours, or longer if cooler.

🕐   If you are not ready to form the dough now, deflate it by pulling the sides toward the center, cover with buttered plastic, a plate, and a weight of some sort, and refrigerate. Push

Sticky dough gradually becomes elastic as kneaded.

It is ready when you can grab and twist it without its breaking.

For kneading by machine, dough is ready when it balls on hook.

down again if it starts to rise before it has chilled and its butter content has congealed. Will keep 12 hours or more.

Final rise in the mold
About 1 hour

Butter inside of mold. Form the dough into a rope 10 to 12 inches (25 to 30 cm) long, rolling it under the palms of your hands, and gradually separating them to extend the dough. Cut crosswise into half, cut each half into thirds, and then halve each third. Drop the pieces into the mold, and press together lightly with your fingers—no need to be too careful since dough pieces will come together as they rise. (Mold should be about half filled with dough.) Cover with plastic and let rise until dough has filled the mold—about 1 hour at 75°F/24°C. (Chilled dough will probably take an hour more.) Meanwhile, preheat oven to 375°F/190°C in time for baking.

🕐 You can delay the rising by refrigerating the mold; you can freeze it. Before baking, let chilled dough come to room temperature; thaw frozen dough and let warm to room temperature.

Baking
About 20 minutes at 375°F/190°C

Set mold in lower middle level of preheated oven. It is done when nicely puffed and browned, and when it comes easily out of the mold. If sides and bottom are not golden brown, return to mold and bake 4 to 5 minutes more. Unmold and let cool upside down on a rack.

🕐 When cool, you may wrap the savarin airtight in a plastic bag and refrigerate for a day or so; it will keep for weeks in the freezer.

The Savarin Imbibes the Syrup:
About 1 hour

Both the syrup and the savarin must be tepid for this step, since a cold savarin will not imbibe easily, and a hot one might disintegrate. If savarin is cold, then, set it in a warming oven or a 200°F/95°C oven for a few minutes. To make the syrup, pour half the water into a saucepan, stir in the sugar, and heat gently until sugar has completely dissolved, then pour in the rest of the water (to cool it); add the rum or liqueur or vanilla. Prick the savarin all over at 1-inch (2½-cm) intervals with a skewer, and set the savarin in a dish. Pour the syrup over it, and dribble the syrup over the top a number of times with a spoon or bulb baster. In several minutes, repeat the process. After about half an hour of frequent basting the savarin will have absorbed all of the syrup; it will look swollen and feel spongy. Transfer onto a rack set over a dish to drain for half an hour, and it is ready to glaze.

🕐 May be done several hours in advance; leave savarin in its dish, and cover with a bowl or with plastic, and refrigerate. Then drain on a rack; if it seems dry, make a little more syrup and baste it several times before glazing.

Apricot Glaze, and Glazing the Savarin:
Heat the apricot jam in a small saucepan with the sugar, stirring until sugar dissolves completely, then boil rapidly, stirring, until jam is quite thick and the last drops falling from your spoon are thick and sticky (the "thread stage," or 228°F/109°C). Push

Let dough (left) rise until it has doubled in volume; it will be light and spongy (right).

As they rise, dough pieces (left) merge to fill the mold (right).

The savarin swells like a sponge as it drinks up the liqueur syrup.

through a sieve to remove skin debris, and return the glaze to the pan.

🕐   If not to be used immediately, set pan in another pan of simmering water; it must be warm or it will not spread. Leftovers may be bottled, reheated, and used again.

Paint the glaze all over the surface of the savarin. Then set the savarin on its serving dish.

🕐   If the glaze has been properly cooked to the thread stage, it should set or jell on the savarin and act as a waterproofing seal; then the savarin can sit for several hours.

Finishing the Savarin:

Cut up the fruits (reserving some of the grapes), toss in a bowl with sugar and, if you wish, rum, liqueur, or lemon juice to taste. To frost grapes, beat the egg whites lightly with a fork to liquefy them, dip in the grapes one by one, roll them in granulated sugar, and let dry on a rack.

Just before serving, pile the fruits into the savarin, and decorate outside with the frosted grapes. To serve, cut wedges out of the savarin, and spoon a serving of fruit on the side. (You may wish to pass additional fruit with the savarin, and a bowl of lightly whipped and sweetened cream, on page 108.)

Variation: Babas au Rhum

Exactly the same dough makes babas, those individual rum-soaked yeast cakes. Use 12 well-buttered baba tins or muffin cups about 2 inches (5 cm) high and 2 inches across, and after the dough has risen in its bowl, form it into a rope, and cut it into 12 even pieces. Drop 1 piece into each cup, let dough rise just above the rims of the cups, and set on baking sheet. Bake about 15 minutes in the middle level of a preheated 375°F/190°C oven. They are done when they unmold easily, and are nicely browned. When tepid, imbibe with the same rum syrup, drain, glaze, and decorate if you wish. Serve as is, with whipped cream, or fruits flavored with the same liqueur.

🕐 *Timing*

This is an easy and relaxed dinner. Fill the center of the savarin with previously trimmed fruit just before you serve it. Before the main course, peel the salmon steaks (a matter of seconds if you chose the fillet, rather than cross-section, type), finish the cucumbers, give the potatoes a toss over heat in their butter, and arrange your platter.

Before sitting down, poach the salmon and leave it in its cooking water. Set the cucumbers in butter over heat, then set aside. Everything can wait off heat while you enjoy the first course. At this time, you can either make the hollandaise sauce (a 5-minute job once you've got the knack), or have it half made and beat in warm melted butter just before serving.

Half an hour before sitting down, start the potatoes boiling.

Several hours beforehand, prepare the fruit for the savarin, and dose the cake with syrup, then glaze it.

Two or 3 days before your party, make the aspics.

The savarin can be baked and frozen long beforehand, or baked the day before and kept in the refrigerator.

One last-minute job—serving the salmon

Menu Variations

Aspic does for any cold food what pearls do for any complexion. Instead of chicken livers, you could use poached eggs—a classic dish—or lobster claw meat poached in wine, or crab, or shrimp, or pieces of *foie gras* and truffle, or liver pâté. Or dress up a cold mousse in an aspic jacket. You might prefer one large mold to individual small ones—though perhaps not a ring mold if you're having the savarin. Decorations, of course, can be very varied; just bear in mind the color of the aspic. Instead of carrots and peas you could use crossed fresh tarragon leaves that have first been dipped in boiling water; or strips of boiled ham, pimiento, black or green or stuffed olives, blanched green pepper, the whites of hard-boiled eggs, and/or the yolks sieved with a little butter and pushed through a paper cone to form designs. Or don't decorate the molds at all; they're handsome as is.

Fish for poaching: if salmon seems too expensive or is unavailable, use some other firm solid fish that has good natural flavor. (Monkfish has the right texture but is altogether too bland.) Halibut and striped bass are delicious poached, as is swordfish. Large cod steaks can take to it but might be more successful in a court-bouillon (a mixture of water, wine, and seasonings simmered for half an hour with 1 or 2 finely sliced carrots, onions, celery, and herbs). Instead of *hollandaise sauce,* you could use melted butter with herbs, or lemon butter or white butter sauces. Dieters could use a decoration of dill sprigs and thinly sliced lemon, more fresh lemon on the side, and perhaps a bowl of sour cream or yogurt brightened with a little mustard, horseradish, fresh pepper, and minced herbs.

Cucumbers are the first thing I think of for salmon, but asparagus, peas, zucchini, or green beans would do very well.

New potatoes are ideal with poached fish, but can't always be had. You might substitute buttered and parslied potato balls, but I don't think any of the richer potato dishes (fried, scalloped, mashed, etc.) would suit. In season, just-picked sweet corn might be nice.

Tradition being what it is, you cannot call anything a *savarin* unless you bake it in the traditional ring mold. But the same dough in another mold will taste the same, and you can call it a rum cake, or a strawberry shortcake if you split it, drench it with strawberry juice, decorate it with sliced berries, and serve it with whipped cream. It is also delicious with rhubarb, sliced peaches, wild berries, and raspberries—for which you might drench it with framboise, the delicious raspberry liqueur. Or have babas!

Leftovers

The *chicken liver aspic* will keep for 2 to 3 days. Or you might buy more chicken livers than you need, make a little extra aspic, and use it to coat a delicious pâté, for which a recipe is included in this section.

For leftover cooked *salmon,* I also include a recipe here, following the one for pâté. Cold poached salmon is delicious with cucumbers and sour cream or mayonnaise, but its beauty is fleeting. Eat it the next day; 2 days later, it'll be better in the nice old-fashioned gratin I've suggested. To stretch it, you can turn it into a sort of kedgeree by adding rice to the mixture.

Leftover *cucumbers* go into soup. But the *new potatoes* can be rinsed of their butter in boiling water, peeled, and used in salad. A slice of cold boiled new potato makes a better carrier than toast for some hors d'oeuvre—for instance, salmon roe with sour cream.

Hollandaise sauce must be discarded if it has sat at room temperature for an hour or more, since it is so vulnerable to bacterial action you can't detect. If it hasn't sat long, you can refrigerate it and reheat it cautiously.

A *savarin* loses its bloom rather quickly, but will still be good the next day. Or you can layer slices of it with custard, to make something resembling an English trifle.

Chicken Liver Pâté

For a 3-cup (¾-L) pâté

1 medium onion

2 Tb butter

2 cups (½ L) chicken livers

4 Tb Port or Madeira wine

½ cup (4 ounces or 1 1 5 g) plain or herbed cream cheese

6 Tb additional butter

½ cup (1 dL) aspic (page 109; or consommé and ½ Tb dissolved gelatin)

Salt and pepper

Herbs and spices: pinch of allspice or special spice mixture (page 109), and/or thyme or tarragon

Cognac or Armagnac in dribbles, if needed

Equipment:

A food processor makes quick work of this; or use a blender, or a sieve and wooden spoon.

Mince the onion and cook slowly in the butter until wilted. Meanwhile, pick over the livers, removing any discolored spots and fat. Stir them into onion and sauté several minutes just until stiffened. Pour in the wine and boil for a moment. Purée the livers with the cheese, additional butter, and aspic. Taste very carefully for seasoning to make a marvelous-tasting mixture, overseasoning a little since it will lose some of its flavor when it is cold. Pack into a mold or bowl, cover, and chill several hours.

*   Will keep for about a week under refrigeration. May be frozen, but will lose something in texture when thawed.

Gratin of Poached Salmon

For 4 people

2 poached salmon steaks (or about 2 cups or ½ L salmon, cooked or canned)

4 hard-boiled eggs

1 large onion

4 Tb butter, more as needed

½ Tb curry powder

5 Tb flour

2 cups (½ L) milk, heated in a small pan

4 to 6 Tb dry white wine or dry white French vermouth

Salt and white pepper

1 tsp or so fresh minced dill weed, or big pinches of dried dill

About ⅔ cup (1 ½ dL) grated Swiss or mixed cheese

Equipment:

A buttered 6-cup (1 ½-L) baking dish 2 inches (5 cm) deep

Flake the salmon, and slice or quarter the eggs. Mince the onion and cook slowly in the butter in a 2-quart (2-L) saucepan; when limp, stir in the curry powder and the flour, adding a little more butter if flour is not absorbed. Cook, stirring, for 2 to 3 minutes. Remove from heat, and let cool a moment, then blend in the hot milk with a wire whip. Return to heat and simmer, stirring, for 2 minutes. Add the wine, and simmer several minutes more, stirring frequently. Season carefully to taste.

Fold the salmon into the sauce, fold in the dill, and taste very carefully again; it should be delicious. Spread half the salmon mixture in the bottom of the buttered baking dish, and spread half the cheese over it. Arrange the eggs over the cheese, and spread the rest of the salmon over them, covering with the remaining cheese.

 Baking dish may be arranged several hours in advance. Cover and refrigerate.

About half an hour before serving, preheat oven to 400°F/205°C. Place dish in upper third level, and bake until contents are bubbling and cheese topping has browned lightly. Do not overcook, or salmon will dry out and eggs will toughen.

Postscript: Hot-weather food

When you think of the foods native to hot climates, like our own gumbos and barbecues and chili, or the curries of India, or the rijstafel of Malaysia, or the tomatoey, garlicky soups and sauces of the Mediterranean, what they seem to have in common is their high, piquant seasoning. It strikes me that hot-weather food should be light but rarely bland; if the appetite is excited, its satisfaction is more intense, and one can do with less. To think that cold food equals light food, however, seems to me an illusion. One double-dip ice cream cone is just as hearty as one steak.

What's called for, I think, is contrast and stimulus: hot and cold, sharp and bland, crunchy and creamy. Before a chicken salad, try a winy consommé, but piping hot, not jellied. And aim for variety. So often, all the dishes on a fancy cold buffet taste mostly of mayonnaise, vinaigrette, cream, and sour cream. One wearies of the ubiquitous lemon: sometime, instead of filling an avocado hollow with oil and lemon, try fresh orange juice spiked with hot pepper sauce. Try horseradish instead of mustard. Try a change of oil: fresh walnut oil, for example, is exquisite.

Our salmon dinner, though it would be nice in any season, seems to me to have a summery air, but temperately so. In *Mastering I*, we devoted a chapter to the classical French cold buffet, and among good cookbooks, all with "summer" in their titles, are Judith Olney's (Atheneum), Molly Finn's (Simon & Schuster), and Elizabeth David's (Penguin).

In extreme hot weather, one can save jobs like baking and simmering for the cool of the evening, or use a hibachi set outside the kitchen door to avoid lighting the broiler. And one's eating as well as one's cooking patterns can be adapted: more for breakfast, and have it earlier, less for lunch, dinner after sundown.

In general, the best rule of thumb is that for dieters' food: in summer, meals should be exciting as well as delicious. Never forget, there was a record heat wave in Fall River, Massachusetts, on that fell morning when Lizzie Borden fetched her axe, and never forget what she had had for breakfast: overripe bananas, too-long-leftover cold mutton, and cookies. No wonder she couldn't keep her cool.

A cool aspic is the perfect start for a summer meal.

An elderly hen, if you treat her right, becomes lady bountiful.

Old-fashioned Chicken Dinner

Menu
For 6 people

*Long Fresh Asparagus Spears, with Oil and
Lemon*
French Bread

❧

*Hen Bonne Femme —A sprightly stuffed fowl
poached whole, and served with onions,
mushrooms, and Sauce Ivoire*
Steamed Rice

❧

Tossed Green Salad
Melba Toast or French Bread

❧

*Bombe aux Trois Chocolats —A chocolate
mousse hidden under a mold of
chocolate fudge cake, topped with
chocolate sauce and a sprinkling of
walnuts*

❧

Suggested wines:
*Although some worthy wine wallahs abstain
from wine with asparagus, I like a light dry
riesling or Sancerre; a full dry white would go
with the chicken, like a Burgundy or
chardonnay, or you could present a light red
Bordeaux or cabernet; sweet Champagne or a
sweet but still wine would go with the
chocolate dessert —a Sauternes, Vouvray, or
gewürztraminer.*

When a hen's too old to lay, she still is useful for something—good eating! Her great egg-producing days are over, and it doesn't pay the poultry man to keep on feeding her. So we feed *on* her, and well, for the great thing about this beldame is her wonderful flavor. Mass produced (battery raised, as some call it), with no exercise and standardized rations, young chickens today don't have the rich taste they used to when they ran around snacking on anything they fancied in the hen yard; but with age and, I presume, experience, they acquire flavor as people do character. Matronly hens taste the way all chicken used to and ought to.

My market says there's not much demand for stewing chickens nowadays, because a lot of customers don't know how to cook them. They treat them like roasters, end up with rubber chicken, and come back to the store mad. But, though you may have to special-order your stewing chicken (or fowl, to be technical), it is available. The demand comes from commercial food processors, and from hotels and restaurants, which use fowl by preference for salads and sandwiches. It's not just because of the fowl's rich taste: hens, not *old* but of a certain age, have an excellent, tender texture when cooked right. The key is long simmering—but not too long, for, just after the point of perfection is reached, utter disintegration sets in and the meat falls flaccidly from the bone. It's curious: the fowl stays obdurately tough for the longest time, then its consistency changes quite quickly; you really have to keep testing.

A "boiled fowl" (gross phrase!) is so useful a resource to have on hand that more households—particularly where everybody goes out to work—should make it a staple.

The next step is so quick and easy, whether you opt for chicken stew, pie, salad, or sandwiches, and the golden broth makes sauce or soup. But don't use a capon or a young chicken or a middle-aged roaster for the purpose. They don't have enough flavor, and long cooking practically dissolves them. (Best moist-cooking method for roasters, in my experience, is the casserole poach, where there is little liquid and the bird steams in a covered pot in the oven, as described in *Mastering I* and *The French Chef Cookbook*.) With a fine fowl (see page 94 for standards of quality), I use a stuffing to bring out the grand flavor, and the broth for sauce (the rest for soup later), and carve before serving. For the price of 3 lamb chops, one can serve from 6 to 8 people, or get at least 3 well-varied dinners for a couple.

Practicality, of course, is something a party should possess but certainly not proclaim! Don't think there is anything humdrum about our "elegant fowl" (as the Owl was addressed by the Pussycat). This is the finest of party food. The full, super-chickeny taste marries so well with a good wine, and the platter looks handsome: smooth-grained meat, ivory satin sauce, and a pretty array of vegetables.

Sauced chicken flanks the stuffing, while mushrooms and onions garnish the platter.

It's an easy dish to serve. And to eat, which can be a consideration. (I remember a very young niece, returning from her first dinner dance in pink tulle—and red wrath. "I'm starved!" she howled. "All the kids are! It was *squab!*" If you have young guests all gussied up in their first party clothes, do feed them something manageable.)

The choice of a first course before chicken is no problem at any time, but in joyful springtime asparagus, for me, is the ideal thing. Is there anything it doesn't complement? (Scallops, maybe—too much too sweet—or a very spicy "made dish" like lasagne . . .) Anyway, the clear fresh green of it and the soft flavor—sweet in the stalk and subtle, vaguely mushroomy, in the tip—are bliss before the sturdy yet delicate chicken. Why before and not with? With is fine, I concede, but consider the sumptuousness, the sheer all-outness, of a whole plateful of nothing but asparagus!—peeled, of course, so the pure green is streaked with ivory. And perfectly drained, and cooked just to the pivot-point between crunchy and soft, and very, very cold—or very, very hot. Rapture . . .

With a bread crumb stuffing and a rich dessert, you don't need bread or rice for starch; but for texture they are nice—fresh French loaf for contrast, or rice for a sauce sopper-up. The salad, with a vinaigrette dressing, is just a hyphen, a refresher.

The dessert on this menu is called Bombe aux Trois Chocolats because it looks like a floating mine and the threat is triple: chocolate mousse encased in chocolate cake, and then, forsooth, coated with more chocolate. (But a little lightly whipped cream, passed separately, softens the chocolate onslaught.) Anybody who comes to this dinner will gaze upon the dark and lustrous dome and know he's at— A Party.

Preparations and Marketing

Recommended Equipment:

Start with one big pot. It's essential that the one for your chicken be deep enough so that the liquid level can be 4 inches (10 cm) above the chicken; stainless steel or enamel is best for cooking with wine, and the pot has to be covered. For asparagus, a large oval casserole or roaster is ideal. For lots of asparagus, a rack fitting the pot (as in a fish steamer) is a nice convenience for lifting out and draining. To truss the chicken, you need plenty of soft white string.

A covered, heavy-bottomed saucepan is a help with rice, and you need 2, preferably 3, more saucepans for sauce, onions, and mushrooms. Onions can, if you like, be precooked and reheated with the mushrooms when you do them.

For the dessert, you need a jelly-roll pan to bake the fudge cake, and a homemade paper pattern or template (which you can file and re-use) as a guide to cutting it. To form the bombe, use a 6-cup (1½-L) bowl, or smooth-sided mold, or even a flowerpot.

Staples to Have on Hand:

Salt
White peppercorns
Granulated sugar
Confectioners sugar
Dried sage
Imported bay leaves
Dried thyme
Whole cloves
Pure vanilla extract
Optional: chicken stock
Gelatin
Butter (3 sticks; 12 ounces or 340 g)
Swiss cheese (2 ounces or 60 g)
Day-old nonsweet white French- or Italian-type
    bread (½ loaf)
Flour
Garlic (2 or more cloves)
Optional: leeks (1 or 2)
Celery (3 stalks)
Carrots (2 medium)
Lemons (1)
Cognac, dark Jamaica rum, or bourbon
    whiskey

A tall kettle is useful for many things, including stewing a chicken.

Specific Ingredients for This Menu:

Stewing chicken (5 to 6 pounds or 2¼ to
    2¾ kg) ▼
Best-quality semisweet chocolate (16 ounces or
    450 g)
Unsweetened chocolate (6 ounces or 180 g)
Walnuts (2 Tb, chopped)
Heavy cream (3¼ cups or 7 dL)
Eggs (7 "large" plus 2 whites)
Parsley (1 good-sized bunch)
Yellow onions (4 or 5 large)
Small white onions (18 to 24)
Mushrooms (1 quart or 1 L), preferably small
Asparagus (36 to 48 spears) ▼
Optional: dry white wine (1 bottle)
Optional: dry white French vermouth (2 cups
    or ½ L), or use more dry white wine

▶ **Remarks:**

Chicken: a good stewing chicken, or fowl, or stewing hen, is just on the shady side of middle age. An "old hen" is great for soup, but too tough to eat. What you want is a bird from 14 to 16 months old, weighing between 4 and 6½ pounds (1¾ and 3 kg), in general—but buy one on the big side to feed 6 amply. She should be plump and chunky-looking; her skin should be white—not yellow; her breast is reasonably full, and her breastbone, if you feel it down to the tip, is not cartilage but solid bone—that shows she's at least a year old. See the introduction to this chapter for more details on this somewhat-neglected—but highly meritorious—type of bird. Since you may have to special-order your fowl, it's worth knowing what to ask for and what you can expect. *Asparagus:* fresh asparagus is sold nowadays from February to June. For information about buying, storing, and preparing, see the following.

Fresh Asparagus

Buying

Fat asparagus is just as tender, in my opinion, as thin asparagus, but I do think you should choose spears all of the same diameter to be sure of even cooking. Pick them spear by spear if you can, choosing firm stalks with closely clinging leaves at the bud ends; the peel from end to end should be tight, bright, and fresh with no creased or withered areas. The butt ends should look moist, and if your grocery store is really serious about asparagus, they will have it standing upright in a tray with an inch of water. Asparagus spears are like flowers: they wilt without moisture.

Storing

When you bring your asparagus home, unwrap it at once, cut a finger width off the butts to reach the moist ends, and it is a good idea to let the asparagus lie for half an hour in warm water, which will refresh it. Then stand the spears upright in a bowl, their butts in 2 inches (5 cm) of cold water, cover loosely with plastic wrap or a plastic bag, and store in the refrigerator. Treated this way, fresh asparagus will stay fresh for 2 or 3 days.

Peeling

There is no doubt at all in anyone's mind who has compared peeled asparagus with unpeeled asparagus—they are two different vegetables. Peeled asparagus cooks evenly from tip to butt in half the time, remains greener, and has a far better texture than unpeeled asparagus. (The same is true of peeled versus unpeeled broccoli.) To peel the spears, you want to take the tough outer skin from the butt end up to near the tip, where the skin is tender. I use a small knife, and lop off a finger width of the butt—or if necessary, I make the cut where the green begins. Then, starting at the butt end, and holding the spear butt up, I start the peel, cutting down to the tender flesh and making the cut more shallow as I reach the tender area near the tip. Using a knife, you can direct the depth of the peel, and it is also good practice in control of the knife. However, you can use a vegetable peeler: hold the spear on your work surface, its butt away from you, and go round and round until you get down to the tender flesh—but be careful holding and turning it, so as not to break the spear.

If you bend an asparagus spear to where it breaks, you are losing a lot of asparagus, whereas a properly peeled spear can be eaten from butt to tip.

Store asparagus with the butts in water; peel just before cooking.

Plain Boiled Asparagus

For 6 people, with 6 to 8 spears per person

36 to 48 fine fresh asparagus spears all the same diameter, peeled

4 to 5 quarts or liters rapidly boiling water

1 ½ tsp salt per quart or liter water

Equipment:

A large oval casserole or roaster; 2 wide spatulas for lifting asparagus out of water; a tray, or rack over tray, lined with a clean towel if asparagus is to be served cold; a platter lined with a double-damask or linen napkin if asparagus is to be served hot

With a small amount of asparagus, there is no need to tie it in bundles for cooking if you have an oval casserole or roaster that will hold it comfortably so that it does not tumble about as it boils.

Bring the water to the rapid boil with the salt, lay in the asparagus, and cover the casserole just until the water begins to boil again—the sooner it reaches the boil, the greener the asparagus; but the casserole must be uncovered while the asparagus is actually boiling—again to keep it green.

Boil slowly, uncovered, for 4 to 5 minutes, or just until asparagus spears start to bend a little when lifted. Remove a spear; cut and eat a piece from the butt end to make sure. Asparagus should be just cooked through, with a slight crunch. Immediately remove the asparagus from the water.

To serve cold

Arrange in one layer on the towel-lined tray or rack, and cool near an open window if possible. Serve with lemon wedges and a pitcher of good olive oil, or with vinaigrette or one of its variations, or with mayonnaise.

To serve hot

Arrange on napkin-lined platter and pass lemon wedges and melted butter, or lemon butter, or hollandaise, page 80. Another method, which I always remember delighting in at my grandmother's house, was to arrange the hot asparagus on a rather deep rectangular platter, season it with salt and pepper, pour lots of melted butter over it, and stand small triangles of white toast all around the edge of the platter.

Asparagus is cooked when the spears bend just a little bit.

Whole Stuffed and Poached Stewing Chicken

"Boiled Fowl"

For 6 to 8 people

Herb and Bread Crumb Stuffing:

1 cup (¼ L) minced onions

3 Tb butter

The gizzard, heart, and liver of the chicken (optional)

2 or more cloves garlic, minced

1 celery stalk, minced

1 "large" egg

2½ cups (6 dL) lightly pressed down crumbs from crustless day-old French- or Italian-type nonsweet white bread

½ cup (1 dL) lightly pressed down, fresh minced parsley

½ tsp dried sage

Salt and pepper

½ cup (1 dL) coarsely grated Swiss cheese

For Stewing the Chicken:

A 5- to 6-pound (2¼- to 2¾-kg) fine plump white-skinned stewing chicken, ready to cook

About 6 quarts (6 L) liquid: 1 bottle dry white wine, plus half-and-half water and chicken stock; or chicken stock and water; or water only

Salt to taste (1 tsp per quart or liter if using only water)

2 large celery stalks

2 medium carrots

1 large peeled onion stuck with 2 cloves

1 or 2 washed leeks, or another large onion

1 large herb bouquet (8 parsley sprigs, 2 imported bay leaves, and 1 tsp dried thyme, tied together in washed cheesecloth)

Equipment:

Either a trussing needle and white string, or a lacing pin (for neck skin) and 4 feet (120 cm) of soft white string (butcher's corned-beef twine recommended); a stew pot just tall enough to hold the chicken submerged plus 4 inches (10 cm) of extra room (make it stainless steel or enamel if you are cooking with wine; aluminum can discolor both the wine and the chicken)

Herb and bread crumb stuffing

Cook the onions slowly in the butter until tender and translucent. Meanwhile, peel and mince the gizzard, and add to the onions; then mince the heart, and add to the onions; and finally, when onions are almost tender, mince the liver. Stir it in and cook a minute or 2, just to stiffen. Scrape into a mixing bowl, stir in the rest of the ingredients, and season carefully to taste.

Preparing and stuffing the chicken

Pull any clinging fat out from the chicken's cavity, and make sure the cavity is free of other extraneous bits. For easier carving, remove the wishbone: open skin flap at neck and feel the fork of the bone with your finger, running from top of breast down each side; cut around the 2 tines of the fork and the top, then cut down to detach fork ends at each side. Cut off wing nubbins at elbows. If you wish an automatic basting system and there is enough chicken fat to do so, place fat between 2 sheets of wax paper and pound to a thickness of about ⅛ inch (½ cm). Slip your fingers between skin and

flesh over the breast on both sides, to detach skin, and slide in the fat over the breast meat. Secure the neck skin (below) against the back of the chicken and fold wings akimbo.

Just before cooking it, salt the cavity of the chicken lightly, spoon in the stuffing (picture 1, below), and truss the chicken.

Trussing a Chicken with String:

Sew or skewer the neck skin against the neck end of the backbone, to hold it in place. Provide yourself with a piece of soft white string (butcher's corned-beef twine recommended) 4 feet (120 cm) long and proceed as follows:

2) Set chicken on its back, its tail toward you. Fold the string in half, and place its center under the chicken's tail piece.

3) Cross the string over the top of the tail piece.

1

4) Bring one end of the string from its side of the tail piece *under* the end of its opposite drumstick, then up over it, and down toward the side of the tail piece from which it came. Repeat the same movement from the other side.

5) To close the vent and bring the drumstick ends together, pull the 2 ends of string away from the sides of the chicken.

Turn the chicken on its side.

6) Fold the wings akimbo, wing ends tucked against the back of the neck. Bring the end of string nearest you along the side of the chicken and on top of the folded wing on the same side, then under the wing, coming out at the back again from under the armpit. Repeat with the string on the other side—along side of chicken, over top of wing, under it, and back again under armpit.

7) Pull both string ends tight across back to hold the chicken in form, and by doing so you will make the wings stand out akimbo to brace the chicken when you turn it breast up. Tie the string ends together at one side of the backbone.

Note: You may have to sew or skewer the vent opening closed if you have a loose stuffing, but the string truss is often sufficient to hold everything in place.

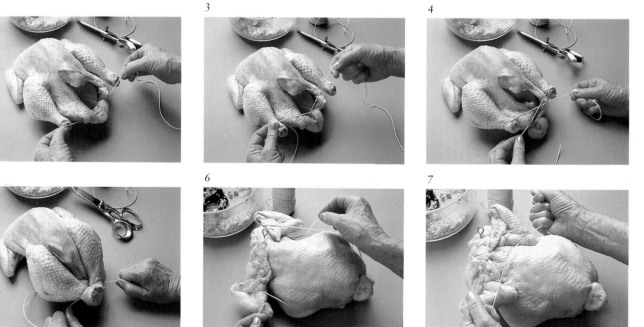

2   3   4

5   6   7

Chicken should be stuffed only just before cooking, since stuffing may start to spoil (especially because it contains bread crumbs), and that will spoil the whole chicken, resulting in a nasty case of food poisoning for all who dine upon it.

Poaching the chicken
2 ½ to 3 hours
Place the chicken in the pot and pour on enough liquid to cover it by 3 inches (8 cm). Add the specified amount of salt, cover loosely, and bring rapidly to the simmer. Skim off gray scum that will continue to rise for 5 minutes or more, then add the vegetables and herb bouquet. Maintain at the slow simmer, partially covered, for 2 hours. (A hard simmer or boil will break the flesh apart.) Add water if liquid evaporates to expose ingredients.

Chicken is not done until a sharp-pronged fork will pierce the large end of the drumstick easily. For 2 hours or more, flesh will be rubbery; then, suddenly, it will become tender, and it should be tested frequently, at 7-minute intervals, when the time might be close. Drumstick meat will just begin to fall from bone when chicken is done; white breast meat will hold, but be tender. Do not overcook.

Chicken will stay warm in its pot for 2 hours or more, partially covered, and may be gently reheated if it cools too much. Chicken should stay in its poaching liquid until serving time; the meat dries out otherwise.

Warning about Covered Pots: Always allow for air circulation, especially when the chicken is not simmering. Cooking liquid and chicken can easily spoil in a nonsimmering covered pot, due to some chemical or bacterial relation between closed containers and warm chicken.

Serving suggestions
The chicken is now ready to be eaten. To serve it cold, let it cool in its cooking liquid and it is ready for salads and sandwiches.

Here is one way to serve it hot:

Hen Bonne Femme

Poached stewing chicken with onions, mushrooms, and white-wine sauce

For 6 to 8 people

The preceding poached stuffed chicken
18 to 24 small white onions
1 quart (1 L) small fresh mushrooms
1 ½ tsp fresh lemon juice

For White-Wine Velouté Sauce (sauce suprême—sauce ivoire):
4 cups (1 L)

About 6 cups (1 ½ L) degreased chicken cooking stock
2 cups (½ L) dry white French vermouth or dry white wine
5 Tb butter
6 Tb flour
½ cup (1 dL) heavy cream
Salt and white pepper
Drops of fresh lemon juice as needed

Braised White Onions:
Drop the onions into a saucepan of boiling water, boil 1 minute to loosen skins, and drain. Shave tops and bottoms off onions, peel them, and stab a cross in their root ends to discourage bursting during cooking. Place in one layer in a covered saucepan with an

Stab roots of onions to prevent bursting.

inch or so of cooking stock, cover, and simmer slowly for 20 to 30 minutes, or until tender when pierced with a knife. They should keep their shape. Set aside, reserving cooking liquid. Reheat before serving.

🕐   May be cooked in advance.

Stewed Mushrooms:

Trim ends off mushrooms. If they seem dirty, drop into a bowl of cold water, swish about, and immediately lift out into a colander. Or wipe them off with a towel. Place in a stainless-steel or enamel saucepan with several spoonfuls of chicken cooking liquid and 1½ teaspoons lemon juice. Toss mushrooms with the liquid. Cover pan and simmer 3 to 4 minutes, until just tender. Set aside, reserving cooking liquid. Reheat just before serving.

🕐   Best not cooked much more than half an hour in advance so the mushrooms will not darken, although you may prepare them for cooking several hours before and refrigerate in dry paper towels and a plastic bag.

The White-Wine Velouté Sauce:

Boil the chicken stock and wine slowly in a stainless-steel or enamel saucepan until reduced to about 4 cups or 1 liter. Melt the butter in a separate enamel or stainless-steel saucepan, blend in the flour, and stir over moderately low heat until butter and flour foam and froth together for 2 minutes without turning more than a buttery yellow. Remove from heat, and when this *roux* has stopped bubbling, pour in a ladleful of the hot chicken stock and vigorously beat to blend liquid and *roux;* blend in another ladleful, and when smooth pour in all but a ladleful. Beat in all but a spoonful or so of the onion and mushroom cooking liquids. Bring sauce to the simmer, stirring, over moderately high heat and simmer 2 to 3 minutes—if you have time, let sauce simmer half an hour or so, stirring frequently; longer cooking will only improve its flavor. Stir in the heavy cream and simmer a few minutes longer; carefully correct seasoning with salt and pepper, adding lemon juice to taste. (Sauce should be just thick enough to coat a wooden spoon nicely, meaning it will just coat the chicken; thin out with chicken stock or cream if necessary. To thicken, boil slowly, stirring, to concentrate it.)

🕐   May be made an hour or so in advance—add the mushroom juices before serving in this case. To prevent a skin from forming on the surface, lay plastic wrap right on top of the sauce, leaving air space at 2 or 3 places around the edge of the pan.

Serving the chicken

At serving time, remove the chicken from the pot to a carving board with a curved edge—to catch juices. Cut off trussing string, and remove the leg-thigh assembly from one side—it should fall off easily. Peel off and discard the skin and remove the meat—which will be so tender you can probably use a spoon and fork—and arrange on a hot

If your mushrooms are large, quarter them.

To serve the chicken, first remove leg-thigh sections; after peeling the skin off the breast, carve the meat.

serving platter. Peel skin off breast, and slice breast meat off the now legless side—breast meat may also be so tender it will come off with a fork and spoon. Arrange breast meat at the other side of the platter, and repeat on the second side of the chicken. Spoon out the stuffing and arrange down the middle of the platter, as shown. Arrange the onions and mushrooms around the meat, and spoon some of the sauce over the meat. Serve rest of sauce separately, in a warmed bowl.

🕐 Chicken should be sauced and served as soon as it is arranged on the platter, to prevent meat from drying out.

The Cooking Stock:
You will still have a good amount of fine chicken stock to use in soups and sauces. Simmer the chicken carcass and scraps in it for half an hour or so, strain and degrease it. Store in the refrigerator in a covered container when it is cold, and boil it up every several days, or freeze it.

Variations on the Sauce:
You can have no sauce at all, if you are counting calories: instead, boil down a good quantity of the degreased cooking liquid until its flavor is full and fine, and spoon some of that over the chicken and vegetables, ending with a generous sprinkling of parsley over the chicken itself; pass the rest of the liquid in a warm sauceboat. Or you can be far richer and creamier with your sauce: boil

Assembled platter; the chicken waiting for its sauce

down 4 cups (1 L) degreased cooking liquid with half that amount of dry white wine or dry French vermouth until reduced by half or less, and then boil down with 2 to 3 cups (½ to ¾ L) heavy cream until sauce has thickened lightly; season to taste, adding lemon juice if needed; pour some over the chicken and pass the rest in a warm bowl.

Variations on the Vegetables:
Rather than onions and mushrooms, you might use the kind of vegetables you'd have with the usual boiled dinner—carrots, turnips, cabbage wedges, onions, and potatoes—all boiled or steamed separately in some of the chicken cooking liquid.

Variations on the Chicken Cooking Method:
Rather than poaching the chicken whole, cut it into serving pieces and place the carcass remains, gizzard, and neck in the bottom of a casserole, topped by the dark meat, and ending with the breast and wings; add the same vegetables to the casserole, and enough liquid to cover the ingredients; cooking time may be a little shorter. By the way, I tried out the oven-steaming method in a covered casserole with a stuffed stewing hen, liquid coming up to mid-thigh, wax paper on, and an oven heat of 275–300°F/135–150°C; the breast, wings, and thighs were fine, but the drumsticks dry and strange; the chicken took about 3¾ hours to cook tender. Perhaps the whole bird needed draping in a sheet of pork fat? I have not yet gone into the pressure cooker or slow cooker—they will have to wait for another hen party.

Chicken Pot Pie:
Using the chicken and its sauce and vegetables, turn them into a chicken pie: arrange in a pie dish or casserole, cover with the buttermilk and herb biscuit dough described for the rabbit pie (page 27), and bake in the same way. Baking time is about 30 minutes in a 400°F/205°C oven.

Bombe aux Trois Chocolats

A chocolate mousse hidden under a chocolate-covered fudge cake dome

This is a dessert for true chocolate lovers, and one that's beautiful to look at and fun as well—though not difficult to make. It consists of a chocolate fudge cake, a kind of brownie mixture, that bakes in a jelly-roll pan. When that is cool, you cut it so that it will line a bowl—or a soufflé mold, if you wish—you fill the lined bowl with chocolate mousse and chill it for 6 hours or overnight. Then unmold (it unmolds easily because first you have lined your bowl with plastic wrap), spoon a little melted chocolate on top, sprinkle on a pinch of chopped nuts for decoration, and you have an incomparable combination of three chocolates: the taste of brittle chocolate topping, the crunch of fudge cake, and the smooth velvet of the mousse.

Our cooking team worked on this for weeks. I had for some time been developing a rich dark mousse, trying to duplicate one I had found remarkable at André Surmain's restaurant in Mougins, in the south of France. But we all thought the mousse cake idea was what we were after, so we set our two chefs, Marian and Sara, to work on developing the perfect combination of cake, mousse, and molding technique. They made more than a dozen, which we solemnly tasted, one by one, and voted upon, narrowing the field to 3. Ultimately, this one really took the cake—and it was the cake indeed that made all the difference, because we wanted the contrast in texture vis-à-vis mousse that the solid fudge cake gave us.

Manufacturing and Timing Note:
I find it best to make the mousse first, so it can set a little bit, yet be soft enough to spoon into the lined mold. While the fudge cake is baking and cooling, you can cut out the template, or pattern, that will guide you in lining your bowl or mold with the cake. (Once I got my first template made, I kept it on file so I wouldn't have to go through that fussy fitting of things again.) The recipe here is for a 6-cup (1½-L) bowl of about 8 inches (20 cm) top diameter, which fortunately just works out for the standard rectangular jelly-roll pan that is about 11 by 17 inches (28 by 43 cm). A charlotte mold or even a flowerpot could be used, of course, and either is fine because they are both tall enough for drama.

For the Mousse — Chocolate Mougins

For 4 ½ cups, serving 8 people

12 ounces (340 g) best-quality semisweet chocolate
1 ½ ounces (45 g) unsweetened chocolate
2 ½ tsp plain unflavored gelatin
3 Tb dark Jamaica rum, Cognac, or bourbon whiskey
3 "large" eggs
2 egg whites (4 Tb)
1 ½ cups (3 ½ dL) heavy cream
1 ½ Tb pure vanilla extract
Large pinch of salt
3 Tb sugar

Equipment:

A small covered saucepan for melting the chocolate and a larger pan with water to set it in; a 2-quart (2-L) stainless-steel saucepan for the custard sauce; a very clean bowl and beater for egg whites, which can also serve for chilling the mousse

Flavor Note: This is a very strong, rich, dark, very chocolaty mousse, on the bittersweet side. It consists only of melted chocolate that is folded into a rich custard sauce, and is lightened by beaten egg whites, yet given body with a little gelatin.

Melting the chocolate

Break up the two chocolates and set in the small covered saucepan. Bring 2 inches (5 cm) of water to boil in a larger pan; remove from heat. Cover chocolate pan and set in the hot water. Chocolate will melt while you proceed with the rest of the recipe. Renew hot water if necessary; chocolate should be smoothly melted and darkly glistening.

The gelatin

Measure gelatin into a bowl or cup, pour on the rum or other liquid, and let soften.

Custard Sauce — Crème Anglaise:

Separate the eggs, dropping the whites, plus the extra whites, into the beating bowl, and the yolks into the stainless-steel saucepan. Set whites aside for later. Beat the yolks for a minute with a wire whip, or until thick and sticky; then blend in the cream. Stir rather slowly over low heat with a wooden spatula or spoon, reaching all over bottom of pan, as liquid slowly heats. (Watch it carefully, and do not let it come to the simmer.) Bubbles will begin to appear on the surface, and in a few minutes the bubbles will start to subside. Then watch for a whiff of steam rising — this indicates that the sauce is thickening. Continue for a few seconds until the sauce clings in a light layer to the back of your spatula or spoon. Immediately remove from heat, and stir for a minute or so to stop cooking.

Combining custard, gelatin, and chocolate

At once stir the softened gelatin mixture into the hot custard, stirring until the gelatin has dissolved completely. Stir in the vanilla, then the melted chocolate.

Finishing the dessert

Set the egg white beating bowl over the hot water that melted the chocolate, and stir for a moment to take off the chill (egg whites mount faster and more voluminously when slightly warmed). Beat at slow speed until they are foamy, beat in the salt, and then gradually increase speed to fast until egg whites form soft peaks. Sprinkle in the sugar, and beat until egg whites form stiff shining peaks. Fold them into the chocolate, then return the whole mixture to the egg white bowl, cover, and chill. Mousse should be somewhat set, not runny, when it goes into the cake-lined mold.

❷   If made and chilled in advance, leave out at room temperature until it has softened. Mousse will keep several days under refrigeration or may be frozen.

Note: This makes a delicious chocolate mousse just as it is. Turn the mousse into an attractive dish or individual pots, and serve with bowls of chocolate sauce and of whipped cream.

Kate's Great Chocolate Fudge Cake

Note: This recipe was developed by our Chef Marian's daughter, Kate Morash, when she was only twelve years old, and makes a most superior brownie as well as perfect cake to surround a mousse—it is crunchy-chewy, yet soft enough to bend to the contours of a bowl.

For a jelly-roll pan about 11 by 17 inches (28 by 43 cm)

Butter and flour for baking pan

1 stick (4 ounces or 115 g) unsalted butter

4 ounces (115 g) unsweetened chocolate

1 more stick (4 ounces or 115 g) unsalted butter, cut into 8 pieces

2 cups (380 to 400 g) sugar

3 "large" eggs

1 tsp pure vanilla extract

½ tsp salt

1 cup (140 g) all-purpose flour (measure by scooping dry-measure cup into flour container and sweeping off excess)

Equipment:

A jelly-roll pan and wax paper; a saucepan for melting chocolate and butter, and another saucepan in which to set the first; an electric mixer, or a food processor; a flour sifter; a cake rack

Preliminaries

Preheat oven to 350°F/180°C. Butter the jelly-roll pan (so the paper will stick to it), cut a sheet of wax paper to fit it with 2 inches (5 cm) of overhang at each end, and press into pan. Butter and flour the paper, knocking out excess flour. Measure out all your ingredients.

Melting the chocolate

Set the first stick of butter and the chocolate in their melting pan, and place in the other pan with 2 to 3 inches of water; bring near the simmer and let the chocolate and butter melt together while you continue with the next step.

Hand made or mixer-made batter

Cream second stick of butter with the sugar until light and fluffy. Beat in the eggs one by one, and the vanilla and salt. Stir in the warm melted chocolate mixture, then gradually sift and fold in the flour. Spread the batter evenly into the pan, and bake at once in middle level of preheated oven, setting timer for 25 minutes.

Food-processor-made batter

Or—cream butter and sugar in processor fitted with steel blade; add eggs one by one, then vanilla, salt, and chocolate. Pour in flour by thirds, blending with 2 or 3 on-off flicks. Spread evenly into pan, and set in middle level of preheated oven.

Baking and cooling

Bake about 25 minutes, until set but top is still spongy. A toothpick inserted into the cake should come out with a few specks of chocolate on it. It should be chewy when cool, and you want it to bend a little so that you can mold it into the bowl; do not let it overcook.

Remove from oven and let cool in pan for 10 minutes. Then turn pan upside down over a cake rack and unmold the cake, gently pulling off wax paper. Cool 10 minutes more.

❶ May be baked in advance. When cool, cover with wax paper, reverse back into baking pan, and cover airtight; store in the refrigerator for a day or 2, or freeze.

Brownies

When cool, cut the cake into 3-by-1½-inch (8-by-4-cm) rectangles. Serve as is, or you may glaze them with the chocolate and nuts suggested at the end of the bombe recipe.

Spread the batter with a rubber spatula.

Assembling the Bombe aux Trois Chocolats

The preceding recipes for chocolate mousse and chocolate fudge cake

4 ounces (115 g) best-quality semisweet chocolate

½ ounce (15 g) unsweetened chocolate

2 Tb chopped walnuts

A bowl of lightly whipped cream sweetened with confectioners sugar and flavored with vanilla (page 108)

Equipment:

A chilled serving platter and, if you wish, a paper doily

The template—or cut-out pattern

Whatever you have chosen as a container for molding the dessert, you will need a pattern of cut-outs to guide you in fitting the cake into the container. This is the system we use for our round bowl: a small cake circle for the bottom of the bowl; 7 wedges of cake to rest on the circle and touch the top of the bowl all around with a little space between each wedge, allowing the mousse to peek through its encircling walls of fudge cake. We also have a large circle to cap the mousse, and all scraps of fudge cake go into the center, giving the bombe a little extra sturdiness for its life out of the mold.

Molding the bombe

Before cutting the fudge cake, slice off a ½-inch (1½-cm) border all around the rectangle, since the edges tend to be brittle—these cut-offs make nice little cookie bits to serve another time. Then cut around the pattern.

Line the bowl with plastic wrap (for easy unmolding), and arrange the cake pieces in the bowl, pressing gently in place, best side out, as shown. Pile half the mousse into the bowl, cover with scraps of the cake (leftovers from cutting patterns). Fill with the remaining mousse and place the large circle on top, pressing it down to force the mousse into the bowl and around the cake. Cover and chill at least 6 hours or overnight.

🕐 Bombe may be refrigerated for several days. It may be frozen, and thawed before serving—several hours at room temperature, or a day or more in the refrigerator.

Unmolding

Loosen the bombe from the mold by pulling up on the plastic wrap, then fold wrap down the outside of the bowl. Center the serving platter (with doily if you are using one) over the top of the mold and reverse the two, unmolding the bombe onto the platter. Melt the chocolate over hot water, as described at the beginning of the mousse recipe, and pour over the top of the bombe, letting the chocolate drip lazily and unevenly down the sides. Top chocolate, while still warm, with a sprinkling of the chopped nuts.

Serving

Cut into wedges, like a round cake, and let each guest help himself to the whipped cream.

Keep your paper pattern for the next bombe.

A layer of cake scraps stabilizes the filling.

After the chocolate sauce, chopped nuts top it off.

⏱ *Timing*

This easy dinner allows you lots of flexibility. If guests are late or want to linger over their cocktails, no harm is done. Your first course of asparagus can be either hot or cold, and that is up to you. If cold, you have nothing to do at the last minute, your chicken and vegetables can wait, and you can go in to dinner whenever you wish. (I shall assume that you are serving cold asparagus in what follows.)

Just before the guests arrive, warm the chicken sauce, the onions and mushrooms together, and the rice—use the restaurant trick of having a roasting pan of simmering water on the stove, big enough to hold those three saucepans, each loosely covered. Have the salad in its bowl, covered and refrigerated, undressed but with dressing ready. Warm the bread if it needs freshening.

About an hour before that, test the chicken for doneness; once tender it can sit in its pot for 2 hours or more, just keeping itself warm. Ladle off the broth you'll need from the pot for cooking the mushrooms, onions, and sauce; if you expose the chicken, drape it in washed cheesecloth and baste with broth—cheesecloth should extend down into the broth on all sides and will draw it up like a wick, thus continuously basting the chicken. Make the sauce now, and you can cook both mushrooms and onions—although the onions could have been cooked in the morning. Whip the cream for the dessert.

Four and a half hours before you plan to serve, stuff and truss the chicken, and start it cooking—you could have made the stuffing in advance and have refrigerated it. Peel and cook the asparagus too, and make its vinaigrette sauce. Prepare the mushrooms for cooking now; wrap in dry paper towels and refrigerate in a plastic bag. You might also sauce the chocolate bombe and finish its final decoration, prepare the salad greens, and cook the rice.

The day before your party, take the dessert from the freezer, if you made it beforehand, and set it in the refrigerator to thaw. Or make the dessert now—or assemble it from its thawed, prefrozen components. Just be sure it has 6 hours or more to sit, in the refrigerator.

Menu Variations

Out of *asparagus* season, what would be a fitting preface for boiled fowl? Artichokes vinaigrette would be my choice, or a salad of sliced artichoke hearts with bits of crab or shrimp or lobster. Young string beans, tossed with butter, lemon, and parsley—another attractive idea, or a salad of cold fresh string beans dressed with onion rings and tomatoes. Still another suggestion, and a nicely old-fashioned one, is clear chicken broth made from your fine pot of chicken-cooking stock.

The chicken: rather than stewing it whole, see the suggestions at the end of the recipe. Or add other meats to simmer with it, like beef, pork, sausages, for a super boiled dinner. Or use turkey instead of chicken.

The sauce: in some families melted butter with parsley and lemon is traditional for boiled chicken, as is hollandaise sauce (recipe, page 80). Some like tomato sauce, and some prefer sour cream with mustard and horseradish.

The vegetables: rather than onions and mushrooms, you could serve boiled or mashed potatoes, or braised Jerusalem artichokes, and something green like Brussels sprouts or broccoli or peas. You could arrange the chicken over a bed of buttered noodles, surrounding it with a green vegetable or with broiled tomatoes.

The *dessert:* the chocolate bombe is indeed a rich and now, because of the price of chocolate, an expensive dessert. You could have the pretty filled meringue cases, or *vacherins* (page 32), or the apple-filled burnt-almond and rum-layered gâteau of crêpes on page 50. Other chocolate cakes in other books are the Victoire and the always popular Reine de Saba chocolate-almond cake in *Mastering I* and in *The French Chef Cookbook.*

Leftovers

Asparagus leftovers will be rare, if you have bought 6 to 8 spears per person; they can be used in a salad the next day.

Any leftover *chicken, mushrooms,* and *onions* can be arranged in a buttered baking dish along with leftover *sauce* and perhaps a sprinkling of cheese from your frozen and grated hoard; bake in a hot oven until bubbling and nicely browned on top, and you have another splendid meal. Or put them into a chicken pot pie, as suggested at the end of the recipe. Ground *chicken* can be added to a stuffing for braised cabbage or stuffed vegetables, or can go into the makings of a meat loaf. Salads and sandwiches are obvious choices for *chicken*—great club sandwich possibilities are there, and it's always handy to have a little chicken to garnish a chef's salad or as an inspiration to make a Cobb Salad. The *mushrooms* and *onions* can be reheated in leftover sauce and served another day; or put them into a chicken soup.

There is never any problem with leftover *rice,* since it can be reheated or turned into a salad, or stirred into a soup.

Simmer all *chicken bones* and scraps in the cooking broth to enrich that already delicious brew, and plan to use it for chicken soup or as a general sauce base.

That good old hen is a good provider!

There will be leftovers of *cake,* thank heavens, because it is so rich you won't be serving it in great hunks. You might make more fudge cake, and then you could trim the leftover dessert cleverly, press decorative pieces of fudge cake onto it, and perhaps pass it off as a brand-new *bombe.* It's worth a try, anyway, because it keeps nicely for several days in the refrigerator, or can be frozen.

Postscript: De gustibus nil nisi bonum

I translate this as: somebody likes it, so don't knock it.

Now and then our team throws itself a party, complete with spouses, paramours, and other affiliates; but the other night we threw a plebiscite. We wanted to hear the voice of the people, on the merits of our three competing recipes for a triple chocolate bombe. After butterflied lamb, scalloped potatoes, and a great vat of vegetable salad, the three candidates, each bearing a numbered banner, were paraded forth and tasted. Comment sheets were pinned up on which everyone wrote his or her opinion of each cake.

The cake that appears in this chapter was by far the popular choice. "Excellent," wrote Dick Graff, a visiting vintner, "good contrast in texture (brownielike cake), luscious chocolate." "Clearly, the only serious choice," proclaimed Russ Morash—unswayed, I feel sure, by the fact that his daughter Kate had developed the fudge cake recipe. Nevertheless, the two other candidates won a share of support, though it was of an ambiguous kind. The same cake Herb Pratt called "nice and wet" Dick Graff perceived as "light and spongy"; and the third seemed to me "a bit soft," though a noncook found it "robust," and added, "Grand bouquet, elegant nose." Wine-taster's terms, but the word "nose" does apply in a way. The nose anyone follows in designing a recipe is, ultimately, his own; it has to be. Follow a recipe precisely the first time is my advice. But then, if you don't quite like it, don't lump it. Change it, and suit yourself.

Appendix

Almonds

To blanch and peel almonds
Drop shelled almonds into a large sauce-pan of rapidly boiling water and boil 1 minute, to loosen the skins. Slip the skins off 2 by 2 (using both hands), squeezing the nuts between your fingers. There appears to be no faster or easier way.

To toast almonds
Spread blanched almonds in a jelly-roll or roasting pan and set in the middle level of a preheated 350°F/180°C oven, rolling them about with a spatula every 5 minutes, until they are a light toasty brown. Be careful they do not burn; they will take 15 to 20 minutes to toast. (Even if the almonds are to be ground, they have better flavor if you toast them whole first.)

To grind or pulverize almonds
Grind them ½ cup (1 dL) at a time in an electric blender, or 1 cup (¼ L) at a time in a food processor using the on-off flick technique. Be careful that the almonds do not grind too fine and turn oily. It is always safer, if you are using them in a dessert recipe, to grind them with part of the sugar usually called for—they are less likely to turn into an oily mass.

Cream

Lightly Whipped Cream—Crème Chantilly:
For about 2 cups (½ L)

1 cup (¼L) heavy cream, chilled
½ cup (1 dL) confectioners sugar (optional)
½ tsp pure vanilla extract (optional)
Equipment:
A 2½-quart (3-L) round-bottomed metal mixing bowl; a larger bowl containing a tray of ice cubes and water to cover them; a large balloon-shaped wire whip, or a hand-held electric beater

Pour cream into metal bowl and set over ice. If you are using a whip, beat with an up-and-down circular motion, to beat as much air into the cream as possible. Or rotate an electric beater around the bowl to achieve the same effect.

In 3 or 4 minutes cream will begin to thicken, and has reached the Chantilly or lightly whipped stage when the beater leaves light traces on the surface of the cream—a bit lifted in a spoon will hold its shape softly.

❶   May be whipped in advance and kept over ice, then whipped lightly again before serving. Or you may refrigerate the cream in a sieve lined with damp washed cheesecloth, set over a bowl; liquid will exude into the bowl as the cream sits—will keep reasonably well for several hours.

If you are serving the cream for dessert, sift on the sugar, add the vanilla, and fold in with a rubber spatula just before using.

Crêpes

For making crêpes for Gâteau Mont-Saint-Michel, use the batter ingredients on page 50 and follow the procedure below.
For 18 to 20 crêpes 5½ inches (14 cm) in diameter

1 cup (140 g) flour (Wondra or instant-blending preferred)
⅔ cup (1½ dL) each milk and water
3 "large" eggs
¼ tsp salt
3 Tb melted butter, or sesame or peanut oil

The crêpes—batter
Scoop dry-measure cup into flour container until cup is overflowing; sweep off excess with the straight edge of a knife, and pour flour into a pitcher or bowl. Blend the milk and water into the flour, beating with a whip until smooth (easy with Wondra or instant-blending flour), then beat in the eggs, salt, and butter or oil. Let rest for 10 minutes (an hour or 2 if you are using regular flour) so that flour granules can absorb the liquid—making a tender crêpe.

The crêpes—cooking
To cook the crêpes, heat frying pan or pans until drops of water sizzle on the surface. Brush lightly with a little butter (usually only necessary for the first crêpe), and pour 2 to 3 tablespoons or so of the batter into the center of the pan, turning the pan in all directions as you do so to spread the batter over the bottom surface. (If you have poured in too much, pour excess back into your batter bowl.) Cook for 30 seconds or so, until you see, when you lift an edge, that it is nicely browned. Turn and cook for 10 to 15 seconds more—this second side never cooks evenly and is kept as the non-public or bottom side of the crêpe. Arrange crêpes, as they are made, on a cake rack so they will cool and dry off for 5 minutes or so. When dry (but not brittle!), stack together, wrap in foil, and place in a plastic bag.

❶   Crêpes will keep for 2 to 3 days in the refrigerator. To freeze, it is best to package them in stacks of 6 or 8; either thaw at room temperature, or unpackage and heat in a covered dish in a moderate oven for 5 minutes or until they separate easily.

Note: I used to stack my cooked crêpes between sheets of wax paper or foil, but now that I have learned the cool-and-dry system, I have not found it necessary, even for freezing.

Egg Whites

To Beat Egg Whites:
Preliminaries
Be sure your beating bowl and beater are perfectly clean and free of oil or grease, which will prevent them from mounting. Before you begin it is useful to wipe bowl and beater with 1 tablespoon each of salt and vinegar, which seem to provide a proper mounting atmosphere. If the egg whites are chilled, set beating bowl in hot water and stir for a few minutes until tepid.

Bowls and beaters
Egg whites mount best when almost the entire mass of them can be kept in motion at once. A beater on a stand should be equipped with a large whip that rotates as it circulates rapidly about the bowl, and the bowl should be narrow, and rounded at the bottom. A hand-held beater works well in a stainless-steel or unlined copper bowl — egg whites collapse down the slippery sides of glass and porcelain; again, choose a bowl with a rounded bottom, and not too big a bowl or you cannot keep the mass of whites circulating as you beat. A giant balloon whip beats egg whites beautifully in an unlined copper bowl, but be sure you have a big enough whip for your bowl.

Beating
Besides having a very clean, grease-free bowl, and room-temperature or tepid egg whites, you must also be sure that there is no particle of yolk in the whites, since this also will prevent them from rising.

However you beat them, egg whites should form shining peaks.

For table-model beaters
Start at slow speed until egg whites are foaming throughout, then add a pinch of salt and a large pinch of cream of tartar for every 3 egg whites — these help stabilize the whites after they have risen. Gradually increase your speed to fast, standing right over the mixer to be sure you don't overbeat the whites. Continue until egg whites form little mountains on the surface; stop and test them — the whites should stand up in stiff shining peaks as illustrated. If you are using the whites in a dessert, beat in ½ tablespoon sugar per egg white, which will also help egg whites at once. Time: with an efficient beater, about 3 minutes.

For hand-held electric beaters
Use the same system as for table-model beaters, pretending you are an efficient whirling and rotating electric whip that circulates rapidly all about the bowl. Time: 3 to 4 minutes.

Beating by hand in a copper bowl
Start at slow speed until egg whites are foaming, then beat in a pinch of salt per 3 egg whites. Gradually increase speed to fast, using an up-and-down circular motion alternating at times with several round-the-bowl beats, and continue until the egg whites form stiff shining peaks. Beat in ½ tablespoon sugar per egg white, if you are doing a dessert. Time: 2 to 3 minutes.

Special Spice Mixture

If you don't have a special grinder, use an electric blender for those herbs and spices that are not already pulverized.

2 Tb each ground imported bay leaves, cloves, mace, nutmeg, paprika, thyme
1 Tb each ground dried basil (if fragrant, or else oregano), cinnamon, and savory
5 Tb ground white peppercorns

Wine-Flavored Aspic

For the Chicken Livers in Aspic, page 77
⅓ cup dry Port wine
3 Tb (1½ ounces) plain unflavored gelatin
4½ cups (1 L) clear consommé

Pour the dry Port into a 2-cup (½ L) measure and sprinkle on the gelatin. Meanwhile, bring the consommé to the simmer. Set aside. When the gelatin has softened, in a few minutes, gradually stir in 1 cup (¼ L) of the hot consommé, then stir this back into the plain consommé.

Note: Proportions
Molded aspics: 1 envelope gelatin (1 tablespoon) for every 1½ cups (3½ dL) of liquid.
For jellied consommés: 1 envelope gelatin (1 tablespoon) for every 2 cups (½ dL) of liquid.

Always test out your aspics before using to be sure they are the consistency you wish. Pour half an inch (1½ cm) into a saucer, chill it 10 minutes or so until set, then fork it up to see and taste.

Index